Japan and a Pacific Free Trade Area
By Kiyoshi Kojima

Professor Kojima, an economist of international renown, here proposes the establishment of a Pacific Free Trade Area, comprising the United States, Canada, Japan, Australia, and New Zealand, which would also jointly promote trade and aid with the developing countries of Asia and Latin America. He believes that the Pacific area, broadly construed, will become increasingly important in world trade, and that Japan must play a leading role in expanding commerce both among the developed countries and between them and the developing nations. In this context he also advocates the institution of a Pacific Currency Area.

Although these proposals may appear to be counsels of perfection, even skeptics will find Professor Kojima's discussion of the need for innovative reorientation of existing international trading practices both original and stimulating—as well as based solidly on an intimate knowledge of the problems involved. His use of economic theory is refreshingly apposite, and his statistical analyses demonstrate a striking mastery of the relevant data. To one who agrees that international trade and monetary policies in the post-Kennedy Round world are in flux and need of redirection, this book offers fresh suggestions for positive action.

Kiyoshi Kojima is Professor of International Economics at Hitotsubashi University, Tokyo.

Japan and a Pacific Free Trade Area

Japan and a
Pacific Free Trade Area

KIYOSHI KOJIMA

UNIVERSITY OF CALIFORNIA PRESS
Berkeley and Los Angeles

University of California Press
Berkeley and Los Angeles, California

© Kiyoshi Kojima, 1971

ISBN 0–520–01736–6
Library of Congress Catalog Card Number 70–121187

Printed in Great Britain

Contents

Preface

International trade and monetary policies in the post-Kennedy Round world are in a state of flux, and need new direction. A restructuring of European trade can be anticipated. The North-South problem still awaits an effective solution.

This volume, which has been drawn together from a collection of essays produced over the past five years, focuses on the genesis of the Pacific Free Trade Area idea as a new design for expanding trade and for accelerating economic development both within and between advanced Pacific countries and neighbouring Asian developing countries. The Pacific should become the major centre of world trade growth. Certainly, Japan should play a leading part in trade expansion among developed countries and in extending aid to and fostering trade growth with developing countries.

The editors of *Studies in Trade Liberalization, Essays in Honour of Sir Roy Harrod* and the *Hitotsubashi Journal of Economics* kindly allowed me permission to republish material from their pages. Chapter 1 is a revised version of 'Trade Arrangements among Industrial Countries: Effects on Japan' in Bela Balassa and associates, *Studies in Trade Liberalization: Problems and Prospects for Industrial Countries* (Johns Hopkins Press, Baltimore, 1967). Chapter 2 is an amended version of 'Towards a Theory of Agreed Specialization: the economics of integration', in Maurice Scott (ed.), *Essays in Honour of Sir Roy Harrod* (Oxford, 1970). Chapter 3 incorporates material from two papers: 'A Pacific Economic Community and Asian Developing Countries', *Hitotsubashi Journal of Economics*, VII 1 (June 1966) 17–37, and 'Japan's Interest in Pacific Trade Expansion: PAFTA Reconsidered', *Hitotsubashi Journal of Economics*, IX 1 (June 1968) 1–31 (originally presented to the conference on Pacific Trade and Development held from 11 to 13 January 1968 by the Japan Economic Research Center in Tokyo). Chapter 4 is reprinted

7

from the *Hitotsubashi Journal of Economics*, IX 2 (Feb 1969) 1–12. And Chapter 5 is reprinted from the same journal, X 1 (June 1969) 1–17 (originally presented to the second conference on Pacific Trade and Development held from 8 to 11 January 1969 by the East–West Center in Honolulu).

I am especially grateful for having had the opportunity to join in stimulating discussions of the proposals put forward in this book at successive Pacific Trade and Development conferences for which I have been privileged to act as general chairman. Professors H. W. Arndt, Sir John Crawford, Richard Cooper, Harry Johnson, William Lockwood, Saburo Okita, Hugh Patrick and Robert Triffin all contributed much in this way to the clarification of my ideas.

Since this is the first book I have published in English, I should acknowledge older debts. Professors Kaname Akamatsu, Bela Balassa, A. J. Brown, G. C. Allen, Gottfried Haberler, Roy Harrod, Fritz Machlup, M. C. Kemp and Jacob Viner had a profound influence on the development of my understanding of international economics, and the award of a British Council Scholarship and Rockefeller Foundation Fellowship helped me to broaden my view of international economic problems.

I am especially indebted, in this context, to Dr Peter Drysdale of the Australian National University for devoting his time to going over my English text, and to Mr Ippei Yamazawa for compiling statistical data.

KIYOSHI KOJIMA

Hitotsubashi University,
Tokyo,
August 1969

1 Japan and World Trade Liberalisation

I. *Japan's Position in World Trade*

Changing patterns in Japanese trade

Japan is a small country, with a high population density and an unfavourable resource endowment.[1] Consequently, the Japanese have had to concentrate on the development of manufacturing industries in order to attain a steady growth of income, and specialisation in manufacturing is associated with heavy dependence on foreign trade. In the past, the commodity and the geographical composition of Japan's exports have undergone successive changes in response to rapid shifts in world demand. This, in turn, has required a continuous process of transformation and modernisation in the Japanese economy. Continuation of this process will be necessary for reducing the gap between Western and Japanese levels of industrialisation and per capita income.

In which commodities and with what countries will Japan's trade expand? These are the questions to which the present chapter seeks some answer. As an introduction to this inquiry, information will be provided about changes in the pattern of Japan's trade, the transformation of her production structure, as well as the geographical and commodity composition of her exports and imports. In subsequent sections Japan's comparative advantage in a multi-country set will be examined and the potential impact of multilateral trade liberalisation on her trade analysed. Finally, alternative trade arrangements will be appraised from the point of view of Japan.

The Japanese economy passed through three major stages of growth between the opening of Japan to foreign influences and the Second World War: the first period was from the 1870s to

1900; the second, 1900 to 1931; the third, 1932 to 1942. In each period, the economy underwent successive transformation through the development of some leading sectors: agriculture and mining in the first period; silk and cotton textiles in the second; heavy industries in the third. The development of heavy industries was not completed during the inter-war years, however, and has continued until the present time.[2] The rate of growth of Japanese exports was high throughout the period: 7·5 per cent a year during the years 1881–5 and 1911–13, and 5·1 per cent during 1911–13 and 1938. This high rate of growth was accompanied by shifts in the structure of exports. After the Meiji Restoration of 1868, Japan was an exporter of primary products and importer of manufactures, like most of the presently developing economies. However, between the 1870s and the Second World War, the composition of Japanese exports changed from reliance on food (especially tea) and raw materials, to semi-manufactured goods (mainly raw silk and cotton yarns), and subsequently to finished manufactures.

The Second World War disrupted Japanese trade to a considerable extent. In 1950, exports were only 32 per cent of their pre-war level, which was not attained again until 1958. Exports grew at an average annual rate of 14·8 per cent between 1950 and 1963 – a growth rate 2·7 times higher than that of world trade, and 1·7 times higher than that of world manufactured exports. Nevertheless, despite rapid recovery and expansion since the Second World War, Japan's share in world trade was only 3·6 per cent in 1963 – still lower than the share she enjoyed before the war (which was 4·6 per cent in 1938).

The post-war period may also be divided into three stages: the first was the wake of war devastation between 1946 and 1953; the second, a period of recovery between 1953 and 1959; and the third, a period of normalisation from 1959 onwards. In 1948, exports were only $U.S. 145 million, but they increased markedly during the Korean War and reached $U.S. 1,273 million in 1953. During this period, about four-fifths of the exports were traditional products such as raw silk, silk fabrics, cotton yarn and cotton fabrics. Manufacturing industries recovered in the second period, however, and provided an increasing share of exports. Total exports grew at an annual rate of 17·4 per cent between 1953 and 1959, and surpassed $U.S. 3·6 billion in the latter year.

The growth of exports slowed down somewhat after 1959, but the 11·7 per cent annual rate of increase between 1959 and 1963 was still more than double the growth rate of world exports. By the end of this period manufactured goods accounted for nine-tenths of Japanese exports and within this category the share of heavy manufactured goods and chemicals increased to a considerable extent. Parallel with these developments, the severe import restrictions in effect throughout the post-war period were progressively liberalised.

As to the dependence of the Japanese economy on foreign trade, we find that imports as a percentage of national income expressed in terms of 1913 prices increased steadily from 6 per cent in the 1880s to 21 per cent in the 1920s. After 1930 this ratio declined to 17 per cent, in a large part because of the fall in world market prices of primary products. The expansion of heavy industries may also have contributed to this result since, as we shall see below, the import content of production is considerably smaller in heavy than in light industries.[3]

Following the decline in the volume of trade during the Second World War, the growth of foreign trade has led income growth in Japan. The ratio of imports to national income, expressed in terms of 1958 prices, increased from the low level of 7·3 per cent in 1950 to 18·5 per cent in 1963. During the same period, the share of exports rose from 7·2 per cent to 14·6 per cent. Finally, in 1963, the average ratio of exports and imports to value added to the production of traded goods was 27·5 per cent in Japan.

Despite the rapid increase of foreign trade in the post-war period, the share of imports in Japan's national income remained well below the inter-war level. Among the factors contributing to this result, the shift from light to heavy manufactures in Japanese production and exports should first be mentioned. The import content of exported goods is 26 per cent in the case of textiles, as compared to 16 per cent for chemicals and 6 per cent for machinery.[4] As the share of textiles in exports and in the gross domestic product declined and that of machinery increased, the import content of exports fell from 23 per cent in 1954 to 15 per cent in 1963, and the import–national income ratio also decreased. The increased self-sufficiency in staple food, the shift from consumption of natural fibres to the use of synthetic fibres, and other technical changes of a material-saving character have had a similar influence, while the rapid rise in imports of mineral fuels has been an offsetting factor.

Transformation of the structure of production

Shifts in the pattern of trade have been associated with changes in the structure of production in Japan. In the 1950s, the transformation of the Japanese industrial structure was more rapid than anywhere else in the world. Between 1954 and 1961, the share of agricultural output in the gross domestic product decreased by 7·5 percentage points, the share of mining output fell by 0·9 percentage points, and transport, communications, commerce and banking by 0·8 percentage points, whereas the share of manufacturing output increased by 6·6 percentage points, construction by 1·5 percentage points, and electricity, gas and water supply by 1·1 percentage points. The sum of these negative and positive movements in sectoral shares was 18·4 percentage points, as compared to 14·3 for Italy, 9·1 for the United Kingdom, 7·0 for the Federal Republic of Germany, 5·6 for the United States, and 5·4 for France. Similar results are reached if we consider changes in the shares of thirteen major industries within the manufacturing sector. The sum of percentage changes is 43·8 for Japan, 20·8 for Italy, 16·0 for France, 11·9 for the Federal Republic of Germany, 8·8 for the United Kingdom, and 4·0 for the United States.[5] During this period, Japanese labour productivity rose more rapidly than money wages, and the reduction in labour costs has been accompanied by a rate of increase of exports far exceeding that of any other industrial country. One of the most important factors contributing to the growth of labour productivity has been a high rate of investment and capital accumulation in the Japanese economy. With the ratio of savings to the gross domestic product exceeding 30 per cent, fixed capital per worker approximately doubled between 1955 and 1963. The importation of foreign technological know-how has also played a part in these developments, while the availability of an ample labour supply has supported the rapid expansion. Investments, as well as increases in productivity, have been concentrated in heavy and chemical industries: between 1950 and 1960, labour productivity in heavy manufacturing and chemicals increased at an annual rate of 13·4 per cent, as compared to 7·6 per cent for light manufacturing.

By 1963, the Japanese economy had attained a level of industrialisation comparable to that of Italy, although it still lagged behind the United States and the more developed European countries. While the share of heavy manufactures and chemicals in total value added in manufacturing in Japan approached that in advanced industrial countries, these industries comprised a much smaller share of manufacturing exports in Japan than in other major industrial countries. In 1960, the relevant figures were 46 per cent for Japan, 60 per cent for Italy, 77 per cent for the United Kingdom, 80 per cent for the United States, and 81 per cent for Germany.

The expansion of heavy manufacturing and chemical industries has followed roughly the same course of development as in the larger industrial countries. Domestic demand, first satisfied by imports, encouraged the expansion of domestic production. The expansion of production then led to the exploitation of economies in scale, increases in productivity, improvements in quality, and reductions in costs. As domestic costs reached the international comparative cost threshold, foreign markets were developed, the scale of production was extended further, and costs were reduced again. Thus, the expansion of exports that had originally been made possible by the growth of domestic demand has, in its turn, provided a stimulus to industrial development.

The production of heavy manufactures and chemicals was increasing rapidly during the inter-war period in Japan but exports remained insignificant. After the war, the expansion of domestic demand for industrial equipment and durable consumer goods stimulated the further development of these industries, and also led to increases in exports. First iron and steel, ships and boats, and light machinery, then radio and television sets, automobiles and motor-cycles, as well as heavy machinery, came to be exported. The importance of new

13

commodities in Japanese exports is indicated by the fact that goods whose share in total exports has risen above 0·2 per cent between 1951 and 1963 accounted for 26 per cent of the total increase in exports during the period.

Structure of Japanese trade

Data on the commodity composition of Japanese exports show the increasing importance of heavy manufactures and chemicals. With an annual growth rate of 23·5 per cent between 1953 and 1963 and 24·5 per cent between 1963 and 1968, the share of these commodities in the total exports of Japan rose from 33·9 per cent in 1953 to 49·8 per cent in 1968 (see Table 1.1). Despite a rate of growth of 13·8 per cent and 10·0 per cent respectively, in the two periods, the proportion of exports supplied by the light manufacturing sector declined from 47·0 per cent to 27·2 per cent between the first and last years. In particular, machinery and transport equipment have replaced textiles as the leading export group. Between 1953 and 1968, the share of the former increased from 16·0 per cent to 43·6 per cent, while that of the latter fell from 36·1 per cent to 15·2 per cent.

Much of Japanese imports are industrial materials (37·5 per cent in 1968). Fuels account for another 20·6 per cent, and food for 14·5 per cent, bringing imports of primary products to nearly four-fifths of the total. Japan's industrial development depends upon her ability to import cheap primary products, since almost 100 per cent of her demand for a number of basic materials – such as wool, cotton, petroleum, iron ore and various non-ferrous metals – is supplied by imports. On the other hand, despite rapid increases since 1953, the share of manufacturing imports remains relatively small (27·1 per cent in 1968). The increase in imports of manufactured goods has been concentrated in machinery that is necessary for the modernisation of manufacturing industries.

The geographical distribution of Japan's exports has also undergone considerable changes in the post-war period (see Table 1.2). Developed countries (North America, Western Europe and Oceania) took 51·1 per cent of Japan's exports in 1968 as compared with 30·4 per cent in 1953, while the share of

Table 1.1. Japan's Trade: Commodity Composition and Annual Rate of Growth, 1953–68
(per cent)

Commodity group	Exports					Imports				
	Commodity composition			Annual rate of growth		Commodity composition			Annual rate of growth	
	1953	1963	1968	1953–63	1963–8	1953	1963	1968	1953–63	1963–8
1. Food, beverages, tobacco[a]	9.4	5.3	3.3	9.2	8.3	25.9	16.2	14.5	5.7	11.6
2. Industrial materials	6.4	3.6	0.8	9.2	−12.3	48.8	41.4	37.5	9.0	11.8
2A. Agricultural raw materials[b]	6.2	3.5	0.8	9.1	−11.8	38.7	28.3	24.8	7.4	11.0
2B. Ores and concentrates[c]	0.1	0.1	0.0	10.7	−40.3	10.1	13.0	12.7	13.7	13.4
3. Mineral fuels[d]	0.7	0.3	0.1	6.1	13.6	12.0	18.0	20.6	15.4	17.2
4. Manufactured goods	82.6	90.2	95.1	16.7	20.3	13.2	24.3	27.1	17.7	16.6
4A. Light manufactures[e]	47.0	40.1	27.2	13.8	10.0	1.4	3.7	4.7	22.4	19.5
4B. Heavy manufactures[f] and chemicals	33.9	39.7	49.8	23.5	24.5	10.5	17.4	15.5	16.5	11.5
4C. Metals[g]	1.7	10.4	18.1	11.5	32.8	1.3	3.2	6.9	20.6	32.7
5. Total	100.0	100.0	100.0	15.6	18.9	100.0	100.0	100.0	10.8	13.9

Note: According to the revised classification of S.I.T.C., the coverage of commodity groups is: (a) Sections 0 and 1; (b) Sections 2 and 4 (less 27 and 28); (c) Divisions 27 and 28; (d) Section 3; (e) Sections 6 and 8 (less 67, 68 and 69); (f) Sections 5 and 7; and (g) Divisions 67, 68 and 69.

Source: Japanese Department of Finance, Japan's Foreign Trade Returns.

Table 1.2. Japan's Trade: Market Composition and Annual Rate of Growth, 1953–68
(per cent)

	Exports					Imports				
	Market composition			Annual rate of growth		Market composition			Annual rate of growth	
	1953	1963	1968	1953–63	1963–8	1953	1963	1968	1933–63	1963–8
I. Developed countries	30·4	47·2	51·1	20·9	20·9	53·3	54·4	50·6	11·9	12·4
North America	19·5	29·9	34·2	20·3	22·1	36·8	35·6	32·2	10·9	11·8
Oceania	1·6	4·1	4·2	26·0	19·4	8·4	8·8	8·6	13·5	13·3
Western Europe	9·3	13·1	12·7	19·6	18·3	8·1	10·0	9·8	15·1	13·8
II. Developing countries	69·2	48·2	44·3	10·4	16·9	45·1	41·5	42·9	10·0	14·7
South-east Asia	47·0	29·5	27·8	9·0	17·6	26·3	18·0	15·3	6·7	10·3
Latin America	8·5	6·6	5·7	11·0	15·5	11·0	8·4	7·4	7·0	11·2
Africa	10·1	8·7	7·2	10·9	14·6	2·3	3·9	6·5	17·9	25·8
Middle East	3·5	3·4	3·6	13·4	19·8	5·5	11·2	13·7	18·9	18·6
III. Communist countries	0·4	4·6	4·5	32·4	18·2	1·6	4·1	6·4	19·2	25·0
Total	100·0	100·0	100·0	15·6	18·9	100·0	100·0	100·0	10·8	13·9

Source: Japanese Ministry of International Trade and Industry.

developing countries fell from 69·2 per cent in 1953 to 44·3 per cent in 1968. Within the developed country group, the importance of North America as a market for Japanese exports further increased (the North American share rose from 19·5 per cent in 1953 to 34·2 per cent in 1968). Despite a rapid expansion of trade, Western Europe's and Oceania's shares have not surpassed 12·7 and 4·2 per cent respectively. At the same time, Japan provides only 1 per cent of Western Europe's imports.

Changes in the geographical origin of Japanese imports have been less marked. Developed countries accounted for 53·3 per cent of Japanese imports in 1953 and 50·6 per cent in 1968, whereas underdeveloped countries supplied 45·1 per cent and 42·9 per cent respectively in the two years. However, the relative importance of particular regions changed considerably. Increased imports of mineral fuels and ores helped Middle Eastern and African countries to increase their shares in Japanese imports from 5·5 per cent to 13·7 per cent, and from 2·3 per cent to 6·5 per cent, respectively, while the shares of South-east Asia and Latin America (whose main exports are agricultural products) fell from 26·3 per cent to 15·3 per cent, and from 11·0 per cent to 7·4 per cent, respectively. These changes have resulted in part from a shift in the commodity composition of imports, increased domestic food production, and shifts in the Japanese diet from rice to noodles, bread, butter and cheese. Further, the deficiency in the supply and the relatively high prices of primary products in developing countries with overvalued exchange rates have been contributing factors. This trend has been accentuated following the liberalisation of imports in 1960, since previously quotas were allocated under bilateral agreements generally favouring less developed countries. Importers now prefer to buy from suppliers in developed countries that often provide cheaper and higher-quality products with reliable delivery dates. In particular, Japan's imports of iron ore, copper, soybeans and sugar come increasingly from North America and Oceania.

Another way to approach the problem is to consider changes in the intensity of trade.[6] The intensity of Japan's export trade with another country is measured by the ratio of that country's share in Japanese exports to its share in total world trade less Japan's imports.[7] Similarly, the intensity of Japan's import trade with another country is measured by the ratio of Japan's share in that country's exports to Japan's share in total world trade less imports into the country in question.[8] Thus, an export intensity of more (or less) than 100 indicates that Japan is exporting more (or less) to a particular country than might be expected from that country's share in the world trade total. Likewise, the intensity of Japan's import trade indicates the extent to which Japan takes more (or less) imports from a particular country than might be expected from that country's share in world trade. The intensity of trade is affected, among other things, by geographical proximity, by economic complementarity, and by political and historical ties.

The intensity of Japan's trade with South-east Asia has been declining in the period under consideration; it was 619 for exports and 383 for imports in the years 1956–8, while the corresponding figures are 291 and 272 in the years 1960–2 (Table 1.3). The intensity of export trade with the Middle East and Africa declined too, although a slight increase in import intensities is shown in the case of these areas. Both export and import intensities increased in trade with Latin America, but the level of intensity remained low.

Table 1.3. Intensity of Japan's Trade[a]

	Japan's exports		Japan's imports	
	1956–8 average	1960–2 average	1956–8 average	1960–2 average
Japan–United States	191	218	180	183
Japan–Canada	48	58	83	94
Japan–Australia	102	160	411	427
Japan–Western Europe	26	26	14	12
Japan–South-east Asia	619	291	383	272
Japan–Latin America	81	107	102	105
Japan–Middle East	158	127	245	253
Japan–Africa	231	123	48	64

[a] For definitions, see text.
Source: United Nations, *Commodity Trade Statistics*.

By contrast, the intensity of Japan's export and import trade with the United States and Australia is high and rising. Increases are shown also in the intensity of trade with Canada, although this has not yet reached the 100 level. In general, Japan's trade has shifted away from the developing countries of South-east Asia to the developed countries of the Pacific area. Trade intensities with Western Europe, however, are the lowest of all, and have not changed substantially during the period under consideration.

II. *Japan's Comparative Advantage in the Multi-country Set*

Comparative advantage in manufactured products

An examination of Japan's comparative advantage is necessary in order to evaluate the possible effects of trade liberalisation among the industrial countries on the pattern of her trade. Professor Balassa suggests that information on relative export and import performance may be used as an indicator of comparative advantage, since these reflect revealed comparative advantage, or the extent of success (or failure) in exporting and importing different commodities.[9] Such success or failure, it is argued, will be determined by relative costs as well as by non-price factors.

Indices of relative export performance and export–import ratios have been calculated for the years 1953–5, as well as for 1960–2, in regard to 74 categories of manufactured goods. Moreover, composite indicators have been derived to reflect the level of these indices in the second period as well as changes over time. The results show Japan to have relative advantages in exporting footwear, cotton yarn and fabrics, clothing, pottery, as well as buses and trucks, while she appears to be at a disadvantage in the manufacturing of aircraft, tractors, wrought nickel and zinc, essential oils and chemical products.

But these indices do not tell the full story. In a country such as Japan where the structure of exports is rapidly changing, it is of interest also to compare the pattern of relative advantages between the two periods under consideration, and to indicate

19

the direction of change. For this purpose, we have divided the 74 commodity categories into three broad groups: S = a strong advantage group (with an index of export performance over 150); M = a medium advantage group (with an index of 67 to 150); and W = a weak advantage group (with an index of 67 or less).[10]

In the first period, Japan had 19 commodities in the strong advantage group, 15 in the medium advantage group, and 40 in the weak advantage group. Between the first and second periods, 6 commodities moved down from the S group to either the M or W group, while 6 commodities moved up from the M group to the S group, so that 19 commodities remained in the S group in the second period. At the same time, the number of commodities in the M group increased from 15 to 20, and those in the W group declined from 40 to 35.[11] The industries which produce commodities that remained in the S group may be called *established export industries*. Except for ships and boats, and universals, plates and sheets of steel, they produce light manufactures (textile products account for 9 of the 13 items) of the traditional kind. Within this category, a decline in relative export performance is shown for cotton fabrics, synthetic fabrics, blankets, special textile fabrics, clothing, made-up textile articles, pottery, jewellery, and universals, plates and sheets of steel, while the opposite conclusion holds for unbleached cotton yarn and thread, miscellaneous woven textile fabrics, floor coverings, as well as ships and boats.

The second group of *established but declining export industries* includes 6 product groups that moved down from the S group to the M or W groups between the two periods. These are wool yarn, synthetic yarn and thread, manufactured fertilisers, simple forms of steel, textile machinery and glassware. All of these products except the last derive from old, established industries in Japan. The trend has been for exports of these commodities to give way to exports of more sophisticated manufactures in the same line, as in the case of special steel products, and to products at higher levels of fabrication, such as the export of wool and synthetic fabrics instead of yarn and thread.

There are 44 *developing export industries* that may, in turn, be subdivided into three groups. The *rapidly developing export industries* moved from the M (or even the W) group to the S group. Both heavy and light industries are represented in this group. Rubber tyres and tubes, railway construction material, buses, lorries and trucks, automobile parts, railway vehicles, electrical machinery other than electrical generators, as well as scientific, measuring and controlling instruments are classified as the products of heavy industry. In turn, footwear, musical instruments and phonographs, travel goods and handbags, fur clothing, and bleached cotton yarn and thread are the products of light industry.

A second group of 15 *developing export industries* moved from the *W* to the *M* group. Most of these commodities come from heavy manufacturing and chemical industries: organic chemicals, plastic materials, a variety of forms of steel, electrical generators, sanitary, plumbing and heating equipment, office machinery, motor-cycles and bicycles, as well as explosives. They also included a few commodities from light industries: leather manufactures, materials and articles of rubber, paper articles and woollen fabrics. Finally, a third group of *slowly developing export industries* improved their export performance but remained, nevertheless, in the *W* group. Of the 16 items in this category – inorganic chemicals, perfumes and cosmetics, medical and pharmaceutical products, leather, fur skins, paper and paperboard, lead, tin, passenger motor-cars, tractors, aircraft, power-generating machinery, metal-working machinery, agricultural machinery, furniture and photographic supplies – the majority derive from the heavy and chemical industries.

Six commodities came from *unsuccessful export industries* that experienced a decline in their export performance. These include chemicals such as synthetic organic dyestuffs, pigments, paints and varnishes, miscellaneous chemical materials and products, and essential oils and perfume materials, as well as glass and machinery other than textile machinery. Finally, five other items which moved down to the *W* group represent a rather special case. They are all semi-processed metals – aluminium, copper, pig-iron, zinc and nickel – and, as industrialisation progressed, the domestic demand for these products increased, and they are now exported in more sophisticated forms.

The data give some indication of the transformation and diversification in Japan's manufactured exports which was characterised by increased reliance on heavy manufactures and chemical products. Three important qualifications should be made to this observation. Firstly, Japan's strongest comparative advantage still lay, in the early 1960s, in textiles and other traditional light manufactures, although there appeared to be a shift from low-quality to high-quality products, as well as from lower to higher levels of fabrication within this category. Secondly, changes within the group of heavy manufactures and chemicals were complicated and diverse. Shipbuilding was already an established export industry in the first period. A number of heavy and chemical products moved into the S group, others expanded their exports but remained in the M or W groups, while some industries experienced a deterioration in their export performance. Thirdly, it should be noted that most of the heavy industrial and chemical product groups are characterised by product differentiation, hence their exports and imports often increased in a parallel fashion. This is not the case for several light manufactures and for metals which are standardised commodities.[12]

Global comparative advantage

The preceding analysis was confined to a study of Japan's comparative advantage in manufacturing exports among ten major industrial countries. Since Japan's trade depends heavily upon imports of primary products and trade with developing countries, it is necessary to study Japan's comparative advantage over a much broader range – not only in manufactures, but also in primary products, and not only commodity by commodity, but also country by country. To simplify the analysis, all commodities traded internationally were classified into four broad groups: the A group consists of agricultural products such as staple and processed foodstuffs, tobacco and agricultural raw materials; the N group includes natural-resource-intensive products outside of agriculture, such as minerals, metals and fuels; the L group comprises labour-intensive manufactures, principally from light manufacturing industries but also from heavy and chemical industries (cameras, sewing machines, bicycles, precision equipment, medicine); finally, the K group encompasses capital-intensive heavy manufactures and chemicals.[13]

22

Fig. 1.1 indicates the composition of exports and imports for the United States, Western Europe, Japan, South-east Asia and the entire world. The percentage share of each commodity group in total exports and imports is represented by the length of the blocked areas in each diagram. Exports are shown on the right and imports on the left of each vertical axis. The staircase

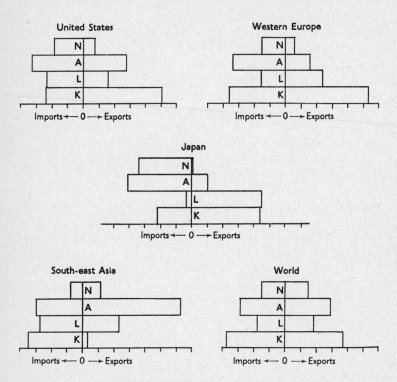

Figure 1.1: Commodity composition of trade, 1960–2 average, shown in per cent.
Source: Japanese Ministry of International Trade and Industry.

shapes of these blocked areas reflect global comparative advantages in each region's trade with the rest of the world.

The simplest pattern on the export side is revealed in the case of Western Europe where the share of N goods in total exports is smallest, and this share increases for A goods, L goods and K goods progressively to make a triangular pattern. If this is

23

compared with that for world trade, it is easy to discern the typical pattern of comparative advantage for highly industrial countries which have the strongest comparative advantage in K manufactures, a lesser advantage in L goods, and a comparative disadvantage in primary products.

The pattern of imports into developing countries is expected to be symmetrical with that of exports from advanced industrial countries. Aside from agricultural products, this is the case in South-east Asia, where the large share of agricultural imports is explained by American aid provided in the form of foodstuffs under the P.L. 480 programme. At the same time, the countries of South-east Asia derive over 60 per cent of their export earnings from the sale of agricultural commodities, chiefly raw materials.

Some differences between United States and European trade patterns should next be noted. The United States exports more A goods in relation to L goods and imports more L goods in relation to K goods than does Western Europe. This reflects the United States' comparative advantage in agricultural and capital-intensive products, and Europe's relative advantage in labour-intensive and capital-intensive manufactures. In comparison with the United States and Western Europe, Japan's trade pattern reveals specialisation in manufacturing industry, and the dominance of imports in N and A goods. L and K manufactures are of approximately equal importance in Japanese exports, while the latter predominate in the exports of the United States and Western Europe. But the share of K manufactures is increasing in both the exports and the imports of Japan, indicating the expansion of horizontal (competitive) trade. These goods constituted 35 per cent of exports in 1956–8 and 44 per cent in 1960–2, and 19 per cent and 22 per cent of imports for the same years.

The pattern of bilateral trade

We indicated earlier that Japan's overall intensity of exports was large in the case of the United States and South-east Asia, was in the intermediate range in the case of Australia and Canada, and was quite low in the case of Western Europe.

24

An examination of the intensity of Japan's exports of particular commodities into each trading region may now be undertaken.

Fig. 1.2 shows the commodity composition of Japan's trade with the United States, Western Europe and South-east Asia. Further, export–import ratios were derived for Japan's bilateral

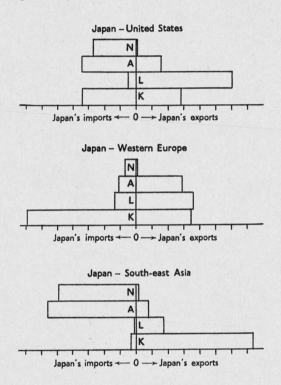

Figure 1.2: Commodity composition of Japan's trade with the United States, Western Europe and South-east Asia, 1960–2 average, shown in per cent.

Source: Japanese Ministry of International Trade and Industry.

and total trade in regard to four commodity groups (see Table 1.4). While the overall ratio rose between 1956 and 1962,[14] Japan continued to run an import surplus in trade with the United States, Canada and Australia, and an export surplus with Western Europe and South-east Asia.

Table 1.4. Export–Import Ratios in Japan's Trade
(per cent)

Upper row = 1956–8 average
Lower row = 1960–2 average

	N goods	A goods	L goods	K goods	Total
Japan–United	1	23	812	25	49
States	1	21	836	56	66
Japan–Canada	3	9	14,467	51	45
	0·1	7	5,666	81	50
Japan–Australia	0·4	1	2,379	52	16
	0·4	2	1,871	151	31
Japan–Western	14	250	312	40	101
Europe	4	302	307	55	110
Japan–South-east	4	10	10,385	11,578	145
Asia	4	15	1,394	2,208	107
Japan–World	1	19	1,462	141	76
	1	20	1,246	158	83

Source: United Nations, *Commodity Trade Statistics*.

In L goods, Japan has a substantial export surplus in trade with all regions. She also has an overall export surplus in K goods, inasmuch as large exports to South-east Asia more than counterbalance her import surplus in trade with the United States, Canada and Western Europe. In turn, Japan has a large import surplus in N and A goods with all regions, the only exception being trade in A goods with Western Europe.

It is apparent that Japan's bilateral export–import ratios in regard to individual commodity groups tend to be either very large or very small. This reflects the predominantly vertical (complementary) nature of Japanese trade. However, as noted above, horizontal (competitive) trade in K goods is on the increase in Japan.[15] Next, we may compare the right-hand side of Fig. 1.2 with the left-hand side of Fig. 1.1 to indicate the differences in the commodity composition of Japanese exports to particular regions and that of the overall pattern of imports into these regions. More exactly, the index of the *commodity intensity of bilateral trade*, calculated by dividing the share of a given commodity in Japan's exports to a particular country by the share the same commodity has in that country's overall imports,[16] reveals the extent to which Japan's exports to a particular country meet the pattern of the latter's import demand. An index of 120, for example, indicates that Japan's exports of a given commodity have a 20 per cent larger share than the average in the imports of this commodity by a particular country.

As column (a) in Table 1.5 shows, Japanese L manufactures had high export intensities in all markets in 1956–8. The

Table 1.5. Commodity Intensity and Regional Bias of Japan's Bilateral Trade

Upper row = 1956–8 average
Lower row = 1960–2 average

	N goods (a)	N goods (b)	A goods (a)	A goods (b)	L goods (a)	L goods (b)	K goods (a)	K goods (b)
Japan–United States	2	95	53	153	401	126	53	44
	2	80	32	112	255	126	117	68
Japan–Canada	8	268	101	117	291	126	38	54
	7	16	49	81	303	146	44	52
Japan–Australia	2	58	54	65	266	144	38	46
	2	47	40	52	227	137	62	69
Japan–Western Europe	3	170	92	319	299	68	94	76
	2	49	87	300	233	74	96	83
Japan–South-east Asia	26	200	21	40	194	95	90	126
	19	284	26	81	60	35	213	178

Source: United Nations, *Commodity Trade Statistics.*
Notes: (a) Commodity intensity of Japan's trade with particular regions.
(b) Regional bias of Japan's trade.
(For explanation, see text.)

index for these goods was highest in relation to the United States (401), and lowest in relation to South-east Asia (194). Except in the case of Canada, the index for these goods had generally declined by 1960–2. The most notable decline was in the intensity of L exports to South-east Asia, where, in contrast, the intensity of K exports increased markedly from 90 to 213. Light manufacturing industries have expanded in South-east Asia over this period, while these countries required increasing imports of K goods. Incidentally, the intensity of exports in K goods increased in all markets, reaching 117 in the case of the United States. On the other hand, the intensity of exports in

N and A goods remained low, the exception being the exports of A goods to Europe where, though declining, the index remained relatively high.

Then again, we may compare the right-hand side of Fig. 1.2 with the right-hand side of Fig. 1.1 for Japan to indicate the differences in the commodity composition of Japanese exports to particular regions and that of Japan's total exports. An index of *the regional bias in Japan's trade* was also calculated by dividing the share of a given commodity in Japan's total exports to a particular country by the share of the same commodity in her total exports.[17] Since the commodity composition of Japan's total exports reflects her overall comparative advantage vis-à-vis the entire world, the resultant index reveals a bias which stems from the difference between Japan's comparative advantage vis-à-vis a particular trading partner and the whole world. If the index for exports of heavy manufactures to the United States is less than 100, for example, the United States can be said to be in a more advantageous position in exporting heavy manufactures than is Japan, even though both countries may enjoy a comparative advantage in these products vis-à-vis the whole world.

Column (b) in Table 1.5 shows that Japan's exports are biased towards L goods in relation to the United States, Canada and Australia, and towards K goods in relation to the countries of South-east Asia. It appears, then, that Japan has comparative advantage in exporting L goods to developed countries, and in selling K goods to less developed areas. This conclusion is supported by the results of a survey undertaken in 1958, according to which the direct and indirect capital requirements per unit of labour input for Japanese exports to the United States were $U.S. 677, to Western Europe $U.S. 716, to South-east Asia $U.S. 927, and to other less developed countries $U.S. 1,543.[18]

Japan's policy objectives

The data indicate a duality in both the geographical and the commodity composition of Japanese trade. For one thing, Japan's exports and imports are roughly evenly divided between developed and developing countries. For another, her trade with developed countries is characterised by the exchange of light manufactures for heavy manufactures and primary products, while she trades heavy machinery for primary products with the developing countries of South-east Asia. In the following, we will consider the implications of this duality for Japanese trade policy.

The importance of Japan's trade with developing countries should be considered first. We noted that half of Japan's total exports are destined for developing countries. This dependence on markets in less developed areas is not a feature of the trade patterns of other industrial countries. Common Market countries sold only 17 per cent of their total exports to under-developed countries in 1963, the United Kingdom 28 per cent, and the United States 32 per cent.

Japan's need for imports of primary products, and the developing countries' rapidly increasing demand for imports of capital equipment, make the further expansion of trade between them seem a most natural and profitable objective. Markets in less developed areas are particularly important for Japanese exports of heavy manufactures and chemicals. Around 66 per cent of Japan's machinery exports, 79 per cent of her chemical exports, and 60 per cent of her steel exports went to these areas in 1963. Exports to developing countries enable new Japanese export industries to realise economies of scale, reduce costs, improve quality and ultimately gain access to more sophisticated markets. Moreover, increased Japanese imports from developing countries lead to a greater rise in Japanese exports to these countries than is the case with increases in imports from developed countries.[19] But there are certain difficulties involved in the expansion of Japan's trade with developing countries. To begin with, these countries are competitive suppliers of primary imports such as iron ore, coal, copper, soybeans, sugar and cotton with the developed countries of the Pacific area. We indicated that, because of lower prices and shorter delivery dates, Japanese imports of these products have increased more rapidly from developed than from developing countries after the import regulations were liberalised. Japan's trade liberalisation has thus 'turned its back' on less developed countries. At the same time, these countries have encountered balance of payments difficulties and have been induced to seek bilateral reciprocity instead of the traditional triangular settlement. Thus, while Japan used her export surplus with developing countries to pay for her import surplus with developed economies in the past, she cannot expect to increase exports to the former group of countries without commensurate increases in her imports from them.

A further consideration is that the expansion of light industries in developing countries has increased their competitiveness with Japan's own exports. Accordingly, Japan has to continue to transform her industrial and export structure so as to make more room for light manufactures from developing countries in her own and in international markets. Aside from concentrating on the production of high-quality textiles, she has to expand further her production and exports of heavy manufactures and chemicals.

We noted that Japan's trade relations with developed countries are characterised by the exchange of labour-intensive manufactures for heavy manufactures and primary products. These observations apply especially to the countries of the Pacific area (the United States, Canada, Australia and New Zealand) but have to be modified in respect to the countries of Western Europe. Although European import capacity is large (the combined imports of the E.E.C. and EFTA countries were $U.S. 61·7 billion in 1963) as compared with the United States ($U.S. 16·5 billion), the countries of Western Europe take only 1 per cent of their imports from Japan, while nearly one-tenth of United States imports originate in Japan. Japanese exports to Western Europe are confined to traditional speciality goods – canned fish, ceramics, whale oil, silk, pearls, pottery and so on – and her imports from Europe are predominantly capital-intensive manufactures and chemicals. Various influences have contributed to this situation.

Europe is geographically distant from Japan and there is less opportunity for business communication and advertisement, or personnel and cultural exchange, than there is in the case of the developed countries of the Pacific area. Also, Japanese and European trade patterns are largely competitive, and high trade barriers have restrained trade between them. Consequently, mutual trade liberalisation is very desirable, and the

30

Kennedy Round offers an opportunity for the pursuit of this objective. Since there is no complementary trade in primary products between Western Europe and Japan, and their exports of light manufactures are competitive, the expansion of horizontal trade in heavy manufactures and chemicals presents the most promising avenue for the expansion of trade between the two regions.

It appears, then, that trade expansion in both of these directions – to developing and developed countries – requires the acceleration of heavy industrialisation, and the consolidation of competitive power in heavy manufactures and chemicals in Japan. This complicates her approach to trade liberalisation. However, five or ten years should see her heavy industries and chemicals on a sound enough footing, and enable her to join in freer trade and successive tariff reductions without fear. International specialisation within this sector must therefore be encouraged in advanced countries.

Continued heavy industrialisation in Japan is desirable, it should be added, because: first, the growth rate in export demand for the products of heavy industry is highest; second, because labour-intensive manufacturing is becoming increasingly less advantageous for Japan. In recent years, wage increases have begun to catch up with productivity increases, and the Japanese economy is now assuming many of the characteristics of a fully employed economy. The tighter labour market has not only resulted in a faster increase in wage levels, but it has also led to some narrowing of the wage differential between light manufacturing and heavy manufacturing industries, and between small and large-scale firms.

Japan's 90 major export items may be classified into five commodity groups according to wage levels prevailing in each group. Exports from industries in lower wage groups (I and II) increased by 61 per cent during the period 1954–8, and by 37 per cent during the period 1958–62, while exports from industries in higher wage groups (IV and V) increased by 117 per cent in the first period and 275 per cent in the second.[20] The lower wage groups include light manufacturing industries such as textiles, clothing, canned food, toys, ceramics and the like. The wage level in the lower wage groups increased more rapidly than that in the higher wage groups, and the wage differential between the two categories narrowed. Between 1958 and 1962, wages in the first category increased by 25 per cent, compared with an average wage increase of 10 per cent for all manufacturing industry.

As a result, Japanese light manufacturing industries are losing some of their advantages to other exporters. Japanese textiles, for example, have recently encountered difficulty in third markets from increasing competition by exporters from Hong Kong, Singapore, Taiwan, India, Pakistan and mainland China. Expansion of exports of light manufactures from developing countries, however, is of paramount importance in Japan's own expansion of heavy manufactured and chemical exports to those regions.

The opportunity for improvement in technology and cost reduction is also smaller in light industries than in heavy industries and chemicals. Finally, the lower import-content of exports in heavy manufactures and chemicals relative to light manufactures would facilitate accelerated economic growth in Japan by reducing the import/gross national product ratio, thereby lessening balance of payments difficulties.

III. *Impact of Multilateral Trade Liberalisation on Japan's Exports and Imports*

Assumptions for estimating the direct effect of tariff reductions

In the following, we shall present some estimates regarding the possible effects on Japanese trade of multilateral tariff reductions undertaken by the industrial countries. Attention is confined to measuring their immediate or static effects only. The direct effect of tariff reductions on trade in each commodity will depend upon the height of the original tariff, changes in tariff rates, and the responsiveness of demand and supply to changes in price. These influences can be collectively called factor α. In addition, the overall direct effect of tariff reductions will depend upon the importance of each commodity in the composition of exports or imports. This can be called factor β.

All commodities which accounted for $U.S. 10 million or more of Japan's trade in 1960 are taken into consideration, but her trade with Communist bloc countries and some European countries outside the E.E.C. and EFTA is excluded. The coverage is thus 91·7 per cent for imports and 83·4 per cent for exports.

Tariff data are derived from two publications, from P.E.P.'s *Tariffs and Trade in Western Europe* and *Atlantic Tariffs and Trade*, and the Customs Tariff of Japan. Since tariff rates quoted there have not been corrected for reductions in duties under the Dillon Round, they are adjusted downwards by 5 per cent here.

Under the assumption that export prices will remain unchanged,[21] t is the original tariff level, and a is the rate of tariff reduction, import prices will decline by:

$$a \cdot \frac{t}{100 + t}$$

where M is the original import value for each commodity, ΔM the increment in import value due to tariff reduction, and η the price elasticity of import demand:

$$\alpha = \frac{\Delta M}{M}$$

$$= a \cdot \frac{t}{100 + t} \cdot \eta.$$

The factor β is measured by the ratio $M/\Sigma M$ and is the share of each commodity in total imports (ΣM) in the base year. Hence:

$$\alpha \cdot \beta = \frac{\Delta M}{M} \cdot \frac{M}{\Sigma M} = \frac{\Delta M}{\Sigma M}$$

and this expression simply indicates the importance of an increment in the import of a particular commodity in relation to the total value of imports.

The increment in Japan's export trade (ΔX) resulting from tariff reductions by other developed countries can be estimated in a similar fashion.

Following estimates by Ball and Marwah,[22] the relevant import demand elasticities are assumed to be as follows:

	For U.S.A.	For other developed countries
Crude foodstuffs	– 0·61	– 0·34
Manufactured foodstuffs	– 2·91	– 1·87
Crude materials	– 0·53	– 0·26
Semi-manufactures	– 1·89	– 1·38
Manufactures	– 4·74	– 3·50

Differences in the tariff structures of developed countries are the most important cause of differences in the value of α. In October 1964, Japan's unweighted average tariff level was 16·2 per cent. This was higher than the E.E.C.'s (11·7 per cent) but lower than similar tariff levels for the United States (17·8 per cent) and the United Kingdom (18·4 per cent).

From the point of view of the potential expansion of exports following reductions in duties, the commodity and the country composition of her trade provide important advantages for Japan. In trade with industrial economies, the share of manufactured goods is greater in Japan's exports (86 per cent), and smaller in her imports (43 per cent), than is the average proportion for the industrial country group (64 per cent). Since tariffs on manufactures are considerably higher than on industrial materials, Japanese exports will tend to rise more than imports.

Within the manufactured goods category, the exports of Japan are concentrated in textiles and other products of light industry which are generally subject to high duties, while machinery and chemicals bear heavily on her imports. Moreover, the United States predominates in Japan's trade with the industrial countries, and by reason of the small share of imports in domestic production, United States import demand is greatly responsive to price changes. In 1960, over 70 per cent of Japanese exports of industrial materials and manufactured goods, destined for the industrial nations, found markets in the United States.

Effects of tariff reductions on Japanese trade

It is estimated that Japan's total imports would increase by 4·6 per cent if her tariff rates were reduced linearly by 50 per

34

cent (see Table 1.6). The impact is so slight because Japanese importing, as already described, is confined largely to raw material supplies on which tariff rates are very low. Imports of primary products would only increase by 0·8 per cent in relation to their 1960 value (the α factor) and by 0·7 per cent in relation to total imports in 1960 (the $\alpha \cdot \beta$ factor). Though increases in imports of manufactured goods would be large (19·1 per cent) in relation to their 1960 value, this would represent only a 3·9 per cent increase on the total value of imports for 1960, since the share of manufactured goods in total imports (i.e. β) is small (20·5 per cent). The effect on particular industry groups may be great despite this small overall impact. In fact, heavy and chemical industries would account for the largest part (82 per cent) of the increase in total imports, and imports of these goods would rise by 19·4 per cent on their 1960 value. Since β for light manufactures is very small (1·2 per cent), increased imports of these products would not be significant in relation to total imports in 1960 (0·2 per cent).

Table 1.6. Estimated Direct Effects of the 50 per cent
Tariff Reduction upon Japan's Imports

Commodity group		North America	Australia and New Zealand	Western Europe	Developing countries	Total
I. Primary products	ΔM	7,779	1,218	427	17,876	27,300
	α	0·66	0·35	0·93	1·06	0·83
	β	28·83	8·38	1·12	41·14	79·47
II. Light manufactures	ΔM	4,961	–	2,770	33	7,764
	α	18·95	–	11·71	5·09	15·38
	β	0·63	–	0·58	0·01	1·22
III. Heavy manu-	ΔM	96,309	2,671	48,976	6,125	154,081
factures and	α	20·58	16·23	20·14	9·07	19·38
chemicals	β	11·37	0·40	5·90	1·04	19·31
Total	ΔM	109,049	3,889	52,173	24,034	189,845
	α	6·49	1·08	16·68	1·36	4·59
	β	40·83	8·78	7·60	42·79	100·00

Notes: ΔM = Estimated increase in imports for each item and area by 50 per cent tariff reduction (thousand U.S. dollars).

$\alpha = \Delta M/M$: percentage rate of increase in imports in relation to the 1960 imports of each item and area (per cent).

$\beta = M/\Sigma M$: percentage composition of 1960 imports (per cent).

The geographical distribution of increased imports resulting from a 50 per cent tariff reduction would be quite uneven. Japan would increase her imports from North America by $U.S. 109 million (a 6·5 per cent increase on the 1960 value of imports from that area) and she would increase her imports from Western Europe by $U.S. 52 million, an increase of 16·7 per cent. However, Japan's imports from developing countries would rise by only 1·4 per cent and from Australia and New Zealand by 1·1 per cent. Generally speaking, imports would increase most from countries who export chiefly manufactured goods to Japan, and least from countries whose exports to Japan were predominantly primary products.

According to our calculations, Japanese exports would rise by 10·4 per cent in the case of a 50 per cent all-round tariff reduction (see Table 1.7). This rate of increase in exports (more than twice that estimated for imports) derives largely from the importance of manufactured goods (90 per cent) in Japan's export basket.

Japan's exports of primary products would increase by 6·0 per cent on their 1960 value under this stimulus. In relation to total 1960 exports this increment is, none the less, negligible since primary exports were a very small proportion of total exports. Exports of manufactures would rise by 10·8 per cent on their 1960 value, and since these goods dominate Japan's basket of exports, they would account for 95 per cent of the total increases in exports. Increases would be larger in light manufactures ($U.S. 239 million or 14·6 per cent) than in heavy manufactures and chemicals ($U.S. 96 million or 6·5 per cent). The concentration of light manufactures relative to heavy manufactures and chemicals in Japanese exports to developed countries (54 per cent of the total as compared with 31 per cent) would make for the more significant expansion in exports of light manufactures.

The United States would absorb most of these increased exports ($U.S. 268 million or 76 per cent of the total increase). This would represent a 28·6 per cent expansion on the 1960 value of Japanese exports to the United States. Exports to Canada and Oceania would rise by smaller amounts ($U.S. 21 million and $U.S. 27 million respectively), but these increases imply 21·0 per cent and 17·6 per cent gains on the 1960 value

36

of exports to those regions. Exports to Western Europe would rise by $U.S. 35·6 million, but this represents only a 10·4 per cent expansion of trade to that area over 1960 values. The differences in these rates of increase derive from the difference in commodity composition of exports and tariff structures by region' and the larger elasticities of import demand assumed for the United States.

Table 1.7. Estimated Direct Effects of the 50 per cent
Tariff Reduction upon Japan's Exports

Trading region

Commodity group		North America	Australia and New Zealand	Western Europe	Developing countries	Total
I. Primary products	ΔX	8,764	928	7,210	0	16,902
	α	8·56	16·82	5·52	0	6·04
	β	3·00	0·16	3·88	1·26	8·30
II. Light manufactures	ΔX	204,950	16,223	17,774	0	238,947
	α	34·08	17·39	12·88	0	14·58
	β	17·79	2·76	4·08	23·85	48·48
III. Heavy manu-factures and chemicals	ΔX	74,915	10,045	10,654	0	95,614
	α	22·55	18·13	12·81	0	6·51
	β	9·83	1·64	2·46	29·29	43·22
Total	ΔX	288,629	27,196	35,638	0	351,463
	α	27·89	17·64	10·13	0	10·40
	β	30·62	4·56	10·42	54·40	100·00

Notes: ΔX = Estimated increase in exports for each item and area by 50 per cent tariff reduction (thousand U.S. dollars).
$\alpha = \Delta X/X$: percentage rate of increase in exports in relation to the 1960 exports for each item and area (per cent).
$\beta = X/\Sigma X$: percentage composition of 1960 exports (per cent).

Whilst imports of manufactures from developed countries comprise only 18·9 per cent of Japanese total imports, exports of manufactured goods to these countries comprise 38·6 per cent of her total exports. Thus Japan would increase her exports by 22·8 per cent to developed countries whilst her imports from these countries would increase by only 7·0 per cent.

These multilateral tariff reductions would be beneficial to Japan's balance of trade. Exports are expected to increase by $U.S. 351 million and imports by $U.S. 190 million. To take account of the small items in Japan's trade, we may divide these increments respectively by the proportion of exports and imports covered in our estimates. Moreover, the increment in imports may be reduced by 10 per cent to allow for transport costs included in the c.i.f. valuation of imports. Hence, the final increase of exports and imports would be $U.S. 421 million and $U.S. 186 million respectively.

Making similar adjustments, it can be seen that Japan's exports to North America and Oceania would increase by $U.S. 379 million and imports by $U.S. 111 million. Japan's export–import ratio with these regions would consequently improve greatly, from 72 per cent to 87 per cent. This result derives from the nature of trade ties with countries in the Pacific area. Over 75 per cent of imports from these countries are primary products, which would be little affected by tariff reductions, and 80 per cent of exports to them are manufactures, excluding processed foodstuffs, trade in which would be greatly stimulated by tariff reductions.

On the other hand, for precisely the reverse reasons, Japan's trade balance with Western Europe would be adversely affected since exports would increase by $U.S. 43 million and imports by $U.S. 51 million.

Altogether Japan's import surplus from developed countries would be reduced to within 10 per cent of total imports.

Japan's export–import ratio with developing countries would deteriorate slightly since imports would increase a little whilst exports are assumed to remain unaffected by tariff reductions among developed countries. However, even imports of primary products would increase less from developing countries (1·1 per cent) than from developed countries (6·0 per cent), because the tariff reductions envisaged would stimulate trade with developed countries more than trade with developing countries.

It is expected that the direct effects of multilateral tariff reductions would work continuously towards increasing the import–national income ratio (import dependence) both in Japan and in other developed countries through the impetus of reduced trade barriers. Their rate of increase would be smaller for Japan than for elsewhere, the difference roughly corresponding to the ratio of Japan's increases in imports to Japan's increases in exports resulting from the tariff reductions. This implies a continuous improvement in Japan's trade balance vis-à-vis developed countries. To the extent that freer trade would accelerate growth in developed countries (as it has in the E.E.C.), Japanese exports would be further stimulated. This would help reduce Japan's large import surpluses in respect of developed countries and assist with her balance of payments difficulties which have proved the greatest bottleneck to her economic growth by 1967. Moreover, these developments would provide greater scope for increasing trade with developing countries within these balance of payments limitations.

Evaluation of the effects of tariff reductions

It has been suggested above that the direct effects of multilateral tariff reductions on Japan's trading position would include a larger increase in exports than in imports, and a consequent improvement in her trade balance. Increased importing would be by no means harmful for Japan. Its benefits include reduced prices for imported raw materials and consumer goods, and consequently lower costs in domestic manufacturing and the enhancement of welfare. The improvement in her trade balance would be particularly marked vis-à-vis developed countries in the Pacific area. These results are subject to various qualifications, however.

First, there are a number of marginal imports whose trade may expand considerably following reductions in tariffs, although reliable estimates can hardly be prepared. Japan's success in introducing new export items in the post-war period indicates that her exports of such commodities may be stimulated by reductions in duties. In turn, these changes are likely to be of lesser importance in the countries of North America and Western Europe that are established producers of manufactures.

A related consideration is that in conjunction with the shift in exports from the products of light to those of heavy industry, tariff reductions would lead to a larger expansion of Japan's exports of heavy manufactures, chemicals and metals than we have estimated on the basis of the 1960 composition of trade. In this connection, note that the share of these commodities in Japanese exports reached 67·9 per cent in 1968 as compared to 43·2 per cent in 1960.

39

Excepted items in the Kennedy Round of tariff negotiations also affect the expansion of trade. From available information, it appears that the exception lists of the other industrial countries include several products of interest to Japan, among them textiles. Correspondingly, excepted items account for a much larger proportion of imports from Japan (perhaps 30–40 per cent in the United States, 20–30 per cent in the Common Market and the United Kingdom) than in total imports into the major industrial countries (15–20 per cent in the United States and the Common Market, and 5–10 per cent in the United Kingdom). Altogether, these exceptions affect 30 per cent of her exports of heavy manufactures. In turn, it has been reported that the Japanese exception list includes some 40 per cent of imports into Japan.

Finally, attention should be given to the dynamic effects of tariff reductions which are not amenable to numerical measurement. Dynamic effects are related to market size and technological change. The reduction or the elimination of tariffs is expected to give rise to technological improvements by increasing the effective size of the market, as well as through the effects of competition in a larger area. In an economy as large as that of the United States, economies of scale are easily exploited, but the expansion of markets through trade liberalisation is necessary for their wide Japanese exploitation. Although Japan's population is 96 million, per capita incomes are still low in relation to the more advanced industrial countries (less than half of those in Germany and the United Kingdom in 1964). Hence the need for the development of overseas markets if economies of scale are to be fully realised, especially in heavy manufactures and chemical products.

Trade liberalisation and foreign investment

The exploitation of economies of scale and technological improvements following the liberalisation of trade would necessitate the merger of small firms, investment in new facilities, and the introduction of modern techniques in Japan. These developments in turn can be furthered by the inflow of capital and technology. Japan provides an attractive outlet for foreign

40

investment since her labour costs are relatively low and the educational level of the labour force is high.

According to an unpublished survey of the Ministry of International Trade and Industry in the period 1950 to 1964, Japanese firms negotiated 2,786 technological assistance agreements of varying importance. In the same period, capital inflow amounted to $U.S. 3,642 million, nearly 80 per cent of which took the form of loans. Portfolio investment other than loans amounted to $U.S. 687 million, and direct investment to merely $U.S. 218 million. Direct investment has been relatively insignificant because of Japan's reluctance to permit direct investment, except in cases when this entailed the importation of new and advanced technology which could not otherwise be obtained. This Japanese attitude stems from fear of the superior financial power of American firms, and a desire to protect domestic industries from domination by foreign firms.

Foreign capital inflow taken together accounted for only 0·7 per cent of total private investment in the period 1955–9 and 1·9 per cent in the period 1960–3. While the amount was not considerable, technological assistance obtained from abroad as well as foreign capital inflow played an important role in the rapid development of specific activities, particularly in heavy and chemical industries. The import of know-how has been instrumental in lessening the gap between techniques in other advanced countries and those in Japan in the manufacture of motor vehicles and industrial machinery, as well as in initiating the expansion of new industries such as petrochemicals, plastics, synthetic fibres and electronics. Most of the technological assistance came from the United States, which also accounted for 70 per cent of direct investment.

Production which in a large part depends on foreign technology expanded 3·5 times as rapidly as total manufacturing output in this period, and accounted for 90 per cent of the production of heavy and chemical industries. It also contributed to the expansion of exports, and accounted for about 15 per cent of total exports in recent years. In turn, payments for patents, royalties and technological assistance in general have increased rapidly, and amounted to $U.S. 623 million in the fifteen-year period.

Japan is still a capital-scarce economy in relation to her

capacity for growth, and might well take a more liberal attitude towards direct foreign investment of a productive kind. Foreign investment of this kind would bring with it advanced technical and managerial know-how, useful foreign ideas and business practices, and would assist in the transformation and rationalisation of Japanese industry. United States firms are especially likely to increase their investment in Japan, and this would promote horizontal trade between the two nations. Japanese firms, on the other hand, could profitably increase investment in Australia, New Zealand and in less developed areas.

Non-tariff restrictions

The use of non-tariff restrictions in Japan and in other industrial countries is of particular concern for the liberalisation of trade. Non-tariff restrictions make multilateral tariff concessions ineffective as they represent a much more direct and far stronger means for restricting international trade. In trade among industrial countries, these restrictions are of special importance for the exports and imports of Japan. Prior to 1960, all Japanese imports were subject to licence. While licences for the imports of many commodities were easy to come by, they often gave rise to irrational decisions on the part of business and affected, to a lesser or greater degree, the structure of imports.

The liberalisation of these restrictions took place in two stages: the first stage lasted from early 1960 through June 1961; the second, from July 1961 to October 1964, by which time 93 per cent of imports were liberalised.[23] Japan accepted full obligations for the elimination of quantitative restrictions under Article XI of GATT in February 1963; shifted to so-called 'Article VIII status' of the International Monetary Fund on 1 April 1964; and became a member of the Organisation for Economic Co-operation and Development in April 1964.

In the first stage, Japan eliminated restrictions mainly on (1) imports of raw materials and semi-manufactured materials used in domestic manufacturing industries and non-competitive with domestic production, and (2) imports of some machinery and steel in which Japan's competitive power was strong. The share of these items in total imports was 27·3 per cent in 1959.

It increased to 28·4 per cent in 1960, and fell successively to 27·9 per cent in 1961 and 25·9 per cent in 1962. While it is not easy to isolate the effects of liberalisation since the behaviour of imports is influenced by the pattern of economic growth and by the business cycle, it would appear that the removal of restrictions has not appreciably affected the imports of raw materials and semi-manufactures in Japan. Nevertheless, the removal of restrictions brought benefits to Japanese importers. Before liberalisation, businessmen were forced to acquire import licences whenever they had the opportunity to do so, and they often failed to give sufficient consideration to price fluctuations and geographical price differentials. Since then, they have been more able to 'shop around' for imported materials in search of lower prices. In the second stage, import liberalisation was extended to (1) foodstuffs, (2) manufactured consumer goods and (3) capital goods, most of which compete with domestic industries. The share of these items in total imports was 14·0 per cent in 1961; it increased to 16·4 per cent in 1962 and to 18·3 per cent in 1963. Thus, following the removal of restrictions, the imports of these items increased more rapidly than did total imports, although it is difficult to evaluate as yet the full impact of the liberalisation of quotas.

Nevertheless, some estimation of the effect of liberalisation may be worth attempting. For this purpose, we have compared the income elasticity of imports for liberalised and restricted items in five commodity categories on a half-yearly basis.[24] In regard to raw materials and mineral fuels, average elasticities for seven semi-annual periods are 0·92 for liberalised items and 0·98 for restricted items. The corresponding elasticities for semi-manufactured materials (covering nine periods) are 2·00 and 1·99 respectively. Thus, in the case of these commodities whose imports were liberalised first, there is practically no difference in income elasticities between liberalised and restricted items.

For foodstuffs, too, the elasticity for liberalised items (3·84) is only slightly larger than that for restricted items (3·40). On the other hand, there is a large difference between the two elasticities in the case of capital goods (covering five periods) and for manufactured consumer goods (covering three periods). The elasticity is 5·60 for liberalised items and 0·72 for restricted items in the former category, as compared with 6·08 and −0·25 in the latter. But the income elasticities for liberalised items have been declining over time. The relevant elasticities for the first three half-year periods immediately after decontrol are: 4·77, 13·30 and 4·06 for capital goods; 11·26, 7·88 and 1·63 for manufactured consumer goods. Similar changes are not observed in elasticities for restricted imports.

Although our survey is tentative, we find some noticeable differences in the pattern of income elasticities. In the case of imports that compete with domestic production, the average elasticities are shown to be much larger for liberalised than for restricted items, indicating that the quantitative restrictions worked rather strictly and that their removal induced some substitution of liberalised for restricted items. At the same time, it appears that the impact of liberalisation is particularly large in the early period after decontrol but tapers off as the process of adjustment proceeds.

Aside from some pressures upon the balance of payments, the recent stage of liberalisation has apparently had beneficial effects on the Japanese economy. There has been minimal disruption in domestic industries, and the new heavy and chemical industries have been stimulated by the impetus provided by quota liberalisation. In particular, it has made businessmen more confident of their ability to survive international competition, and has also led to the rationalisation of production.

Japan is now proceeding with the third and final stage of liberalisation. Import quotas remained in October 1965 in effect on 162 items of the Brussels Tariff Nomenclature. Among these 162 items, 38 items are generally excepted items under Article XX of GATT, and security exceptions under Article XXI include items such as arms, ammunition, anaesthetics and so on. The remaining restricted items accounted for 10·7 per cent of total imports in 1963. Of these, 1·9 per cent are agricultural products, 5·5 per cent minerals and fuels, 2·4 per cent heavy manufactures and chemicals, and 0·9 per cent other commodities. The principal items are: (1) agricultural products (75 items), including rice, wheat, butter, cheese and meat; (2) minerals and fuels (12 items), of which the most sensitive items are gas, oil and heavy fuel-oil; (3) heavy manufactures and chemicals (52 items), of which the most sensitive items are heavy electrical machinery, electronic computers and machine-tools. These will be reduced to 80 items in January 1971.

Restrictions on the importation of foodstuffs present difficult policy problems for Japan, just as they do for other advanced countries. Abolition of restrictions remains politically difficult since a large number of small farmers would be adversely affected if these restrictions were removed. An economist cannot but conclude, however, that Japan will find it difficult to catch up with Western standards of per capita income unless she liberalises imports of foodstuffs, in particular imports of dairy products, meat and fruits. This is a necessary task, but should be undertaken gradually over a ten-year period (or more). While about 3 per cent of the agricultural working force is being transferred to the manufacturing sector annually, it would be desirable to accelerate this trend.

Similar considerations apply to the restriction of coal and oil imports. The domestic production of petroleum is rather limited, and quota restrictions have been maintained largely to prevent the rapid substitution of oil for coal. However, the protection of coal is hardly justified since this industry produces at high costs in Japan.

Restrictions on the importation of motor vehicles and machines have been maintained for a quite different reason. Business leaders assert that these are still weak and internationally uncompetitive industries, despite the increasing flow of exports from them. The Government remains concerned that liberalisation would lead to a rapid substitution of the foreign for the domestic product, since there is some tendency for the Japanese consumer to prefer the foreign merchandise. It is also assumed that imports would increase rapidly in the future because of the high income elasticity of demand for these commodities. However, the international competitiveness of these industries has greatly increased in recent years, and there is little doubt that quotas could be removed[25] in exchange for similar concessions on the part of Japan's trading partners.

Of the 62 member nations of GATT, 27 use their right under Article XXXV to refuse the application of the Agreement to Japan. As most of these are developing countries, this discrimination does not have substantial adverse effects upon Japanese trade at the present. Japan's most serious concern is the application of quotas against Japanese exports by industrial countries. So called 'voluntary export quotas' are a special form of quantitative restrictions which grew out of difficulties encountered in the rapid increase in exports of a few products (particularly cotton textiles) to the United States in the mid-1950s, and spread to Japan's trade with Canada and Western Europe. The importing countries claimed that the interests of 'orderly marketing' demanded export restraint on the part of Japan, and Japan accepted these demands because she feared the imposition of more stringent trade restrictions. In November 1964, there were 67 items under voluntary quotas in the United States, 28 in Canada, 65 in the United Kingdom, 24 in Denmark, 7 in Switzerland, 5 in West Germany, and 1 item in both France and Norway.

In addition to voluntary quotas, ordinary quota restrictions are imposed in Western Europe against Japanese exports, although successive rounds of negotiations have reduced their importance in recent years. There are such controls on 382 items of the Brussels Tariff Nomenclature in Austria, 119 in Italy, 91 in France, 88 in Norway, 33 in Benelux, 28 in West Germany, and 18 in the United Kingdom. It is estimated that in 1962 these restrictions, including voluntary quotas, affected 14 per cent of Japanese exports to the United States, 23 per cent of exports to Canada, 20 per cent of exports to the Common Market countries, 6 per cent of those to the United Kingdom, and 40 per cent of those to Norway. In Sweden, Denmark and Portugal, all imports from Japan enter under government licence.

The principal items affected by voluntary quota restrictions and other non-tariff measures are: (1) textile products, including clothing (woollen and cotton), synthetic yarn and fabrics, tableware, carpets, as well as footwear; (2) miscellaneous light manufactures of a labour-intensive type, including canned vegetables, fruits, sea foods, buttons, toys, hand-tools, plywood, tile products, china and ceramic ware, etc.; (3) equipment of a labour-intensive type, including electric bulbs, binoculars, bicycles, sewing machines, radios, transistor radios, cameras, insulated electric wire, etc. These commodities can often be produced by Japan at lower cost than they can be supplied by other developed countries.

It should be emphasised that restrictions against many of these imports in developed countries are reserved exclusively or mostly for Japan, while the import restrictions imposed by Japan are global in character. Because of the existence of non-tariff restrictions which operate in a discriminatory fashion against Japan, tariff reductions on certain light-industry products would be quite ineffective in stimulating her trade. In these cases, any gains in trade would accrue to competing suppliers as long as Japanese exports are voluntarily restrained. As mentioned before, items subject to non-tariff restrictions more or less overlap excepted items under Kennedy Round negotiations. This double protection is surely unreasonable.

IV. *The Choice for Japan*

The best choice for Japan is to expand and free her trade with every trading region. The present stage of her industrialisation, her dual pattern of trade with developed and developing countries, and her geographical location dictate such a choice. The continuation of Kennedy Round-type tariff reductions on a multilateral basis would serve this objective reasonably well. Aside from the static benefits of trade liberalisation, a rapidly growing economy in the process of industrial transformation like Japan has much to gain from the dynamic effects of freer trade and capital flows. At the same time, multilateral tariff reductions and the elimination of quantitative restrictions would tend to improve Japan's trade balance vis-à-vis the industrial countries.

But Japan has to give attention to two important problems in promoting trade liberalisation. First, the comparative advantage of Japanese production, and the structure of her trade vis-à-vis developed countries, suggests that tariff reductions would stimulate the growth of light industries more than that of heavy and chemical industries. At the same time, Japan is pledged to heavy industrialisation and aims to develop her heavy and chemical industries more rapidly than her light industries. Nevertheless, although it may be legitimately feared that hasty tariff reductions, as well as decontrol, would stifle the expansion

47

of some immature heavy and chemical industries, in so far as tariff reductions in the Kennedy Round would not become fully effective until the early 1970s, Japan should be able to make the necessary adjustments. Indeed, heavy industrialisation is likely to be accelerated by the creation of larger markets and the freer inflow of foreign capital and know-how. Multilateral tariff reductions may then contribute to increased horizontal trade in heavy manufactures and chemicals with industrial countries.

Second, Japan cannot disregard the interests of developing countries, especially in South-east Asia. The question is often raised: should Japan rely on the rapidly increasing but competitive markets in developed countries, or on the complementary but more slowly expanding markets in developing countries? She has, in fact, to expand trade in both directions. Tariff reductions of the Kennedy Round type would not be contrary to the interests of developing countries, since they would benefit from tariff reductions under the most-favoured-nation clause. But in order to reduce the gap in growth rates between the two groups of countries, tariff reductions will have to be supplemented by the application of other measures, such as the liberalisation of quotas and foreign aid.

At the same time, multilateral tariff reductions among advanced countries would present no political problems for Japan. Internally, they should produce a minimal disturbance – as noted above, heavy and chemical industries would have sufficient time for adjustment – and externally, they fit into the pattern of her established international alliances. Moreover, such an arrangement would not be objectionable to Japan's Asian trade partners who would automatically benefit from tariff reductions under the most-favoured-nation clause.

However, proposals for a North Atlantic Free Trade Area comprising the United States, Canada, EFTA and Japan seem quite premature. Japan considers it necessary to maintain tariffs for the sake of developing her heavy and chemical industries. Moreover, the establishment of a 'rich man's club' in the form of NAFTA would have particularly adverse effects for the developing countries. Given Japan's special position vis-à-vis Asian countries, the price of her membership in a North Atlantic Free Trade Area would be particularly high. The trade-diverting effects of a NAFTA on Japanese imports from Asia

48

would make the expansion of her exports to that area more difficult, and the political disadvantages of turning her back on Asia would be considerable.

Japan's interests in trade lie importantly with the countries of the Pacific region. The countries of this region have intensive and complementary patterns of trade which could be expanded further in the framework of a free-trade area. Japan would benefit through the cheaper imports of raw materials and other primary products, the expansion of her exports of light manufactures, and the promotion of horizontal trade in heavy manufactures and chemicals. Given the possibilities of expanding trade with Australia and New Zealand, Japan may indeed prefer a Pacific Free Trade Area to a NAFTA which may not include the latter two countries. A related consideration is that Japan has greater bargaining power in Oceania than in Western Europe, and that she is destined by geography to participate in political and economic arrangements in the Pacific rather than in the Atlantic region. The establishment of the Common Market and Britain's desire to join the E.E.C. have led both Australia and New Zealand to look increasingly towards neighbouring countries, and especially towards Japan. However, Japanese markets alone are too small for primary produce from Oceania, and the markets of Oceania alone are too small for Japanese manufactures. Hence, the usefulness of a Pacific Free Trade Area would be greatly increased if the United States and Canada also participated in it.

To date, the United States has been more interested in Atlantic arrangements. However, European integration through a fusion of the E.E.C. and EFTA could well produce an 'inward-looking' Europe, whereupon the United States might find closer integration in the Pacific region desirable. And while for the time being the political and economic integration a free-trade area entails is not feasible in the Pacific area, economic co-operation among the advanced countries in the region could be profitably fostered. Collective measures by the group are especially desirable for assisting economic development and trade growth in South-east Asian countries.

It has also been suggested that Japan should consider some form of integration among developing countries of South-east Asia. The ECAFE Secretariat has studied a number of proposals

49

for integration in this area. But, compared with Europe or advanced countries in the Pacific area, countries in South-east Asia are less homogeneous, trade less with each other, and are less disciplined financially; also, there exists considerable political enmity and nationalistic antagonism among them. All this makes regional integration quite unworkable. Co-operation in the form of specific projects in irrigation, transportation and/or subregional integration seems feasible. But even if integration were possible among the less developed countries of the area, Japan's participation would be neither possible nor desirable. Her superior competitiveness in manufacturing industries would tend to stifle the development of competing industries in the less developed countries of South-east Asia. Moreover, Japan alone could not bear the financial burdens that her membership would entail. It would seem far better for Japan, in co-operation with other developed countries, to promote economic development in the region through collective assistance.

Japan is also interested in expanding her trade with socialist countries (the Soviet Union, Red China and Eastern Europe) that provide a marginal, though growing, outlet. The share of these countries in Japanese exports increased from 0·4 per cent in 1953 to 4·5 per cent in 1968; on the import side, the relevant figures are 1·6 and 6·4 per cent. While tariff reductions of the Kennedy Round type would not hurt the interests of socialist countries if these multilateral tariff reductions were extended to them, the establishment of and Japan's membership in NAFTA would not fail to provoke adverse political and economic reactions.

In short, multilateral tariff reductions and the promotion of freer trade among developed countries, either on a global or regional basis, should be among Japan's foremost policy objectives in the coming decade. At the same time, she must join and encourage collective action by developed countries for fostering the growth and trade of developing economies which need special consideration in the process of trade liberalisation.

2 An Approach to Integration: The Gains from Agreed Specialisation

I. *Introduction*

The scope for significant multilateral moves towards free trade in the coming decades is severely limited. The second-best option is for Japan to push freer trade on a regional basis. This book intends to advocate moves towards Pacific economic integration, either through the formation of a Pacific Free Trade Area, a Pacific Currency Area, and a PAFTA Aid-cum-Preference System, or through more gradual but steady progress towards closer trade partnership among advanced Pacific countries (Australia, Canada, Japan, New Zealand and the United States). What is the theoretical foundation for such proposals? Firstly, faced with slow and unsatisfactory progress through multilateral trade liberalisation and international monetary co-operation on a non-discriminatory basis under GATT and within the I.M.F., alternative solutions have to be found. Secondly, the possibility that greater positive benefits are obtainable through regional integration, although it appears to be a 'second-best' detour towards world-wide free trade, also should be explored.

World trade in post-war years has been characterised by a decline in the importance of *vertical trade*, the exchange of foodstuffs and raw materials for manufactured goods, and growth in the importance of *horizontal trade*, the exchange of manufactured goods among advanced industrial countries. These trends have been accompanied by successful moves towards regional integration among advanced industrial countries at a similar stage of economic development within the E.E.C. and EFTA. By most criteria, the economies which have participated in European integration might have been thought highly competitive. Following the success of these moves, less developed countries have become interested or actively involved in similar moves towards regional integration among neighbouring countries at a roughly similar stage of economic development. What are the reasons for these trends in world trade and what is the rationale of moves towards economic integration? How might realisation of the gains from regional integration be facilitated by agreed specialisation?

At the end of a Seminar on Asian Trade held by the Institute of Development Economics, Karachi, in 1961, Sir Roy Harrod concluded that 'it would be worth placing strong emphasis on the general idea of agreed specialisation. This might be put forward to those concerned, as a proposal urgently requiring study.'[1] Earlier he had suggested that the basic idea of agreed specialisation was that

> the advantages of a larger market should be secured, not *ex post* by some tariff manipulation, but *ex ante* by some previous agreement about the directions into which investment should be channelled in each separate country. Thus, the danger of overlapping and of the production of surpluses in the field of manufactures (for example, textiles) might be averted. A larger market might be secured for each industry by a more rational direction of investment resources in the first instance. The nations might authorize each other to specialize, by developing in some particular directions, and thus give each the advantage of the large market afforded by the region as a whole.[2]

The main purpose of this chapter is to examine the concept of 'regional agreed specialisation' as one of the most important potential incentives for developing and developed countries alike to work towards regional economic integration.

II. *World Trade and Economic Integration*

The shift away from vertical trade, which was the predominant pattern in the nineteenth century, towards horizontal trade, which has been fast becoming the predominant pattern since the Second World War, can be explained in terms of shifts in the underlying determinants of comparative advantage.[3]

52

Suppose that goods are produced by the combined input of three factors of production: labour (L), which can be conceived of in the narrow sense of human time availability; natural resources (N), including land, fertility, climate, and other geographic factors; and capital (C), which can be conceived of in the broad sense as comprising social capital, human skills, and technological and organisational knowledge, as well as material capital equipment. The theory of factor proportions (the Heckscher–Ohlin theorem) cannot be applied easily or usefully to the three-factor case, but if one of these three factors can be taken to have no significant influence in determining comparative advantage, some useful generalisations can be made.[4] Three patterns of trade specialisation are then possible, namely, an N-L pattern, a C-L pattern, or an N-C pattern.

Briefly, it can be said that growth in world trade was determined mainly by the N-L pattern of specialisation during the nineteenth century and by the C-L pattern of specialisation after the Second World War. In the nineteenth century, the structure of world trade was determined by the existence of abundant labour with limited natural resources in Britain and huge unutilised natural resources with scarce labour in newly settled regions. The third factor, capital, moved freely and was of no great importance in determining differences in comparative advantage. Natural resources were, of course, fixed in location, so that this N-L pattern of complementary specialisation was stable and brought about the transmission of economic growth through trade expansion.

In the twentieth century, particularly since the Second World War, trade in manufactured goods among industrial countries has grown much more rapidly than trade in primary commodities. Because of the rapid and widespread progress of industrial technology, capital has displaced natural resources as the significant factor in trade growth.[5] Since primary inputs for manufacturing are available at almost the same price for different industrial countries,[6] the N factor can be regarded as making no substantial difference to comparative costs among industrial countries, so that the C-L pattern has become the main determinant of world trade growth.

The shift in world trade expansion from the N-L pattern to the C-L pattern brought difficulties both for primary producing

53

countries and for industrial countries. First, because of the proportionate decline in world demand for foodstuffs and raw materials, the growth of advanced economies no longer transmits itself strongly to peripheral economies. Not only has the transmission of growth through trade expansion almost ceased, but also less developed countries suffer from so-called 'backwash effects',[7] the effect of 'immiserising growth',[8] unstable terms of trade, and declining terms of trade, all of which reduce the attractiveness of development through specialisation in the world economy. In consequence, less developed countries have turned towards policies to foster their own industrialisation. Under these circumstances, there appears a strong case for promoting regional industrialisation among countries which stand on a roughly equal footing, in order to realise economies of scale in manufacturing activity.

Second, the C-L pattern of trade also brought difficulties for advanced industrial countries. Since the C and L factors are variable in the long run, C/L ratios are instrinsically unstable and successive changes in international specialisation between industrial and industrialising countries are inevitable. The closer the C/L ratio between countries, the smaller will be the difference in comparative costs. Competitive economies producing similar commodities without substantial cost differences can easily separate their markets through tariff and other protective measures. Hence, economic integration within the E.E.C. and EFTA was aimed at eliminating protective barriers, stabilising trade in manufactures, and the achievement of economies of scale within a larger market.

The theory of customs union and the associated theory of the large markets set out to explain the gains from economic integration. The question arises, are there additional factors which experience suggests are necessary to realisation of the gains from regional integration?

The theory of customs union focuses on analysis of the static gains from economic integration. Following Viner, if *trade creation* exceeds *trade diversion*, customs union, or the extension of tariff preferences, will be beneficial.[9] On the production side, *trade creation* requires incomplete specialisation prior to integration and the contraction of import-competing industries within the union. *Trade diversion* is consistent with complete

54

specialisation prior to union and involves the redirection of union imports away from lower-cost outside sources of supply towards higher-cost union sources of supply. Thus, the gains from union appear greatest for protection-ridden economies with similar structures of industrial production. As Lipsey suggests, 'the customs union is more likely to bring gain, the greater the degree of overlapping between the class of commodities produced under tariff protection in the two countries'.[10]

There are also potential gains from customs union on the consumption side. If there is substitutability in consumption, customs union may even result in welfare gains where there is Vinerian *trade diversion* on the production side, through the possibility of increased consumption of preferred imports from the partner country.[11] Or there may be welfare losses through a switch away from preferred outside imports to less preferred partner-country substitutes.

Arguments for economic integration which rest upon the existence of favourable *trade-creating* production or consumption effects are as much arguments for general tariff reductions as they are for preferential tariff reductions. Cooper and Massell, for example, rightly point out that the effect of customs union is the sum of two components: '(1) a non-preferential tariff reduction, and (2) a move from this position to a customs union with the initial tariff. This analytical distinction shows clearly that any rise in consumer welfare as a consequence of forming a union, whether the result of trade creation or a favourable consumption effect, is due entirely to the tariff reduction component of the move.'[12] Viner was also quite explicit that *trade creation* is good and *trade diversion* is bad from a free-trade point of view.

What, among other things, traditional customs union theory fails to explain satisfactorily is why a country might be prepared to reduce tariffs preferentially and sacrifice inefficient import-competing industries yet not be prepared to reduce tariffs generally in order to achieve the same objective. This failure derives in part from the one-sector, partial equilibrium nature of much of the analysis of customs union. But it also reflects inattention to the importance and nature of the bargaining process involved in tariff rearrangements. Importantly, partners to customs unions are prepared to reduce tariffs preferentially,

55

and cut back less efficient import-competing production, on the strength of assured gains for efficient export industries in partner-country markets. It appears, then, that some new theory about the way in which these gains can be realised is essential to a more complete analysis of the process of economic integration.

Agreed trade liberalisation is a prerequisite to realisation of the mutual gains from preferential tariff reduction. Commonly, agreement will be premised on assurances from partners to the tariff reduction of reciprocal and approximately equal gains from trade expansion. Such agreement can be seen to constitute the first important element in any concept of agreed specialisation.

Agreed specialisation is a means, then, whereby a group of like-minded countries with similar structures of production can realise static gains from freer trade. Elsewhere, Johnson has suggested another reason for agreed specialisation.[13] He developed a model in which it is assumed that countries have a preference for industrial production. In this model

> ... it is lower-cost satisfaction of the demand for collective consumption of industrial production that is involved, and this can only be achieved through the co-operation (via bargaining) of the other country .... Each country therefore stands to gain, in terms of real income, by exchanging a reduction of its industrial production through its own tariff reduction for an equal expansion of its industrial production through the other country's tariff reduction.[14]

Countries desirous of agreed industrial specialisation have a clear interest in preferential trade liberalisation. They will commonly be weaker industrial economies – stronger industrial economies would have little to fear from multilateral trade liberalisation since their industrial exports are likely to expand more than their industrial imports with general tariff reductions. Preferential trade liberalisation will enable weaker industrial countries to prevent market penetration from the strong industrial countries; to enjoy a more efficient allocation of regional resources, increased production and static trade gains; and to improve their competitiveness through various dynamic effects such as the securing of economies of scale.

Finally, a large market is said to ensure

the full employment of machines, mass production, specialisation, exploitation of the latest technical discoveries, a revival of competition – all these factors tend to reduce production costs and selling prices. In addition there is the possibility of a net reduction of one element of the price through the abolition of customs duties. The result should be an increase of purchasing power and a rise in the real standard of living. The increased number of consumers of a particular product should thus permit an increase in consumption and hence a greater increase in investment.[15]

Economic expansion begins to cumulate.

An enlargement of markets through economic integration undoubtedly increases the scope for large-scale production. And the securing of economies of scale is certainly a primary objective in establishing large markets. But how exactly can the benefits of large-scale production be achieved?

Most economists rely on the effects of increased competition within larger markets to ensure that benefits from economies of scale are secured.[16] Increased competition has two important effects. First, it stimulates the reallocation of resources that yield static gains from economic integration, as marginal producers contract production and shift into more efficient lines of production. Second, increased competition is likely to induce the employment of mass-production methods and the best industrial practices. Scitovsky, for example, argued that economic integration as such may not increase trade among member countries substantially.[17] Increased competition is likely to have its main effect through the adoption of mass-production techniques to supply national markets in effective competition with lower-cost suppliers within the union. This second, dynamic effect, therefore, results from an increase 'merely in competition'.[18]

Of course, greater economies of scale would be obtainable if the larger integrated markets, not national markets, were the target of mass production. But agreement in specialisation would be necessary between partner countries if these were to be achieved. Without agreement, location theory suggests that

57

increased competition is most likely to result in the agglomeration of industries in particular areas.[19]

Moreover, the stimulation of increased competition is attainable through non-discriminatory trade liberalisation at least equally as well as it is through discriminatory trade liberalisation.[20] The case for regional integration rests on the logic, therefore, that economies of scale can be achieved within a larger integrated market and competitive power improved through union *but that* it is also beneficial to resist the pressure from more competitive producers outside the integrated market. A plausible theory of economic integration must spell this logic out in some detail.

III. *A Model of Agreed Specialisation*

What should be the principle of the international division of labour within a large integrated market? Is some special theory necessary to explain the gains from market integration?

Many economists would argue that reallocation of resources within the member countries of an economic union should follow the usual principles of comparative advantage and that no special theory is required to analyse the changes consequent upon union.[21] This is correct once integration has been set in motion and in so far as the static reallocation of resources is the only important effect of integration, although some agreement will be necessary even to effect tariff reductions and ensure a fair share of the static gains from specialisation among participating countries. Johnson has already explored this question, so it is not the main concern here. But a new theory of agreed specialisation does appear crucial to an understanding of how the dynamic gains from regional specialisation can be achieved.

The benefits of specialisation through the achievement of economies of scale in different lines of production will require agreement among the participants in an economic union.

Assume that long-run decreasing costs characterise industrial production. The production function can be written:

$$P = T \cdot f(C, L) \tag{1}$$

58

where P stands for output, C for capital, L for labour and T for the level of technology.

The level of technology chosen can be supposed to depend upon the size of the market:

$$T = \phi(M) \qquad (2)$$

where M represents the size of the market; ϕ is an increasing function, or $\partial T/\partial M > 0$, and has a limit at the maximum level of technology T^*. Note that the size of the market is dependent upon the nature of competition within the industry as well as the volume of national output, since the degree of monopoly or extent of oligopoly clearly affects the size of the market for each producer. Note also that the function relating the level of technology and market size is likely to be a stepped non-continual function, since indivisibilities of plant and equipment are likely to be prevalent.

Assume a two-country model in which country 1 and country 2 initially produce two commodities x and y. Production functions are of the type described above and the same as between countries but different as between industries. Productive factors are identical but immobile internationally and technology is known in both countries. Prior to economic integration, assume that there was no trade, or negligible trade, between the countries because of the existences of tariff or other protective barriers. Each country adopted the most profitable level of technology in relation to its domestic market size and the prevailing degree of competition. Country 1 employed technology T_x^i and T_y^i appropriate to the size of the market for each commodity M_{ix} and M_{iy}. Country 2 employed technologies T_x^j and T_y^j appropriate to the size of its markets M_{jx} and M_{jy}.

Suppose there is economic union between two such countries through which tariff and other trade barriers are removed and commodity prices equalised in both national markets, transport costs being assumed insignificant. The integrated market for each commodity will be larger than each separate national market, since

$$M_{tx} = M_{ix} + M_{jx}$$

and
$$M_{ty} = M_{iy} + M_{jy}.$$

59

Hence, it will be feasible for a superior level of technology, T_x^i and T_y^i, to be adopted within each of the integrated markets, M_{tx} and M_{ty}, if the two countries can agree to specialise in the production of one or the other of the two commodities. If, for example, country 1 agreed to concentrate on the production of x and country 2 on the production of y, the two countries would be able to achieve economies of scale, increased output and higher economic welfare. Thus, agreed specialisation primarily aims at securing improved production methods in both countries and dynamic gains from trade specialisation. These

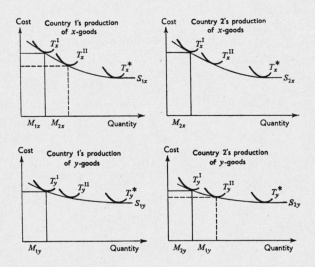

Figure 2.1: The gains from agreed specialisation: a partial equilibrium model.

dynamic gains from trade specialisation are different in kind from the static gains from specialisation which merely involve the reallocation of resources with a given level of technology.[22]

Fig. 2.1 describes the foregoing argument diagrammatically. T^I, T^{II}, ..., T^* are short-run supply curves corresponding to various levels of technology related to market size. The long-run supply curve, S, is an envelope of these short-run curves.[23] Prior to economic integration, both countries of similar market size employed technology T^I and produced x and y at cost levels represented by the unbroken lines. After integration, agreement on complete specialisation is reached between the two countries, whereby country 1 produces a larger volume of x for the combined market in countries 1 and 2 at a lower cost, shown by the broken line, through shifting from technology level T_x^I to T_x^{II}. Similarly, country 2 specialises in the production of a larger output of commodity y at a lower cost by shifting from technology T_y^I to T_y^{II}. Here, the gains from agreed specialisation are shown by the reduced costs, in terms of costs per unit of commodity and total resources required to meet the pre-union level of demand in both countries taken together.

The logic of agreed specialisation appears simple. But some further explanation is in order. First of all, why is agreed specialisation a prerequisite to the realisation of these gains? Significantly, agreed specialisation is necessary because of the nature of the market for industries subject to decreasing costs of production.[24] It is widely held that 'if economies of scale are internal to the unit of production, monopoly will establish itself and . . . one country will exploit the other monopolistically or else there will be bilateral monopoly and indeterminacy', and therefore that 'analysis in terms of competition is applicable only if we suppose the diminishing costs to be due to external economies'.[25] Let us assume, following Meade, however, that 'the economic system behaves as if there were perfect competition', an assumption justified by further

assuming *either* that the economies of scale are external to the individual firms and that there is a system of taxes and subsidies which equates price to marginal social cost in each competitive industry, *or* that economies of scale are internal to large monopolistic firms and that the State controls each industry in such a way that it produces up to the point at which the price is equal to the marginal social cost of production.[26]

To begin with, assume a model in which the two integrating countries are identical, possessing the same factor endowments, production functions, market size and tastes. If there are economies of scale in industries x and y, the transformation curve will be convex to the origin as shown in Fig. 2.2. Let A

61

represent the origin for country 1 and B the origin for country 2; then the transformation curves MaN for country 1 and MbN for country 2 are identical. Further, assume identical production functions in each industry so that the lengths of the vertical and horizontal axes are the same and the transformation box $AMBN$ is a square.

On the demand side, make some additional simplifying assumptions as a reference point. Social preferences are depicted by homothetic indifference curves which will be symmetric with respect to the 45° line. This implies not only that the income elasticity of demand for each good is unitary but also

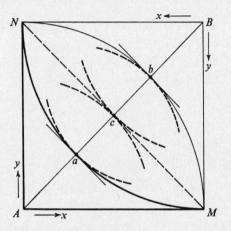

Figure 2.2: Possibility of agreed specialisation: a general equilibrium model.

that the propensity to consume each good is the same and equal to one-half. That is, both goods will be consumed equally with unitary relative prices at all levels of income. The nature of homothetic indifference curves also implies that the 'contract line' will be the diagonal AB.

Now it follows that one of the indifference curves in each map will be tangential to country 1's transformation curve at such a point as a and country 2's transformation curve at such a point as b, both on the contract curve AB. These are the pre-integration equilibrium positions for each country and they are stable equilibria, since the convexity of the indifference

62

curve is greater than the convexity of the transformation curve. The pre-integration relative price lines, which are tangential to both the transformation and consumption curves at a for country 1 and b for country 2, will be parallel to each other and intersect the contract curve at right-angles. Neither of these completely identical countries has any comparative advantage in producing one or the other commodity and there is no price incentive to specialise and trade. This conclusion is quite independent of the existence of trade barriers between the two countries.

It is usually argued that with decreasing costs, whatever the terms of trade, each country should specialise completely. For it is clear that if the terms of trade are more favourable to commodity x (or y) than the slope of the line connecting the extremities of the production frontier, consumption possibilities are highest if all resources are devoted to the production of x (or y).[27] This is applicable to both countries. As can be seen from Fig. 2.2, either the two countries specialise completely at M, where country 1 produces AM of commodity x and country 2 produces BM of y, or they specialise completely at N, where country 1 produces AN ($=BM$) of y, and country 2 produces BN ($=AM$) of x. In either case, international equilibrium is attained at c, where the consumption indifference curves of the two countries are tangential to each other on the contract curve, and the equilibrium terms-of-trade line, McN, is parallel to the initial domestic price relatives for both countries and at right-angles to the contract curve. Thus, complete specialisation either at M or at N will bring about large and equal gains for both countries in this reference model.

It has been shown that, although there is initially no price incentive for the two countries to specialise and engage in trade, the realisation of economies of scale through specialisation would clearly be beneficial to both countries.[28] It is, indeed, the specialisation itself which creates comparative advantage. How can two such countries achieve these advantages from specialisation? There is no price incentive, so the price mechanism will not be effective in encouraging the benefits from specialisation. An agreement to specialise in order to realise these dynamic trade gains *would* be effective.

It emerges that trade liberalisation *per se* might be a relatively

63

insignificant element in agreed specialisation, since the existence of two such identical economies in which there are opportunities for gains from integration does not depend on the prevalence of tariff protectionism. Free trade is necessary to the achievement of gains once agreement has been reached, specialisation begun, and comparative advantages revealed. On the other hand, it is also clear that without agreement, development through regional integration would result in the agglomeration of industrial activity.[29]

Where partners are completely identical, as shown in Fig. 2.2, it is of no consequence which partner specialises in the production of which commodity. In either case, complete specialisation would yield equal gains for both countries and leave the terms of trade the same as they were before integration. Under these circumstances, there is no basis for conflict in reaching agreement on specialisation. In most circumstances, however, the gains from trade are likely to be unequally distributed; and the more unequally they are distributed, the more difficult it will be to reach agreement on specialisation.

(i) Some of the assumptions of our reference model can now be relaxed in order to explore these possibilities. First, assume that all other assumptions remain unchanged but that the propensity to consume one of the two commodities is higher, say two-thirds for x and one-third for y.[30] Inspection shows that in this case, the equilibrium terms of trade will be more favourable to x than the slope of the line MN in Fig. 2.2, connecting the extremities of the production frontier, so long as demand is elastic with respect to price. Although the total output of both countries together is the same whether they specialise at either extremity of the production frontier, total demand in both countries increases more for commodity x than for y under unitary relative prices. Hence, both countries would prefer to specialise in the production of commodity x. That is not to say that specialisation at extremity M or N would not benefit both countries. But there would be divergent gains from trade. For example, at M country 1 would specialise completely in the production of commodity x and obtain greater gains from trade than country 2. Agreed specialisation would be more difficult to arrange. The inequality of gains would have to be compensated for within a more comprehensive type of agreement. In practice, of course, as the number of pairs of commodities being traded increases, the inequality of gains resulting from agreed specialisation in one pair of commodities is able to be offset by reverse inequalities for other commodities, and agreement will be thereby facilitated.

(ii) Now, let all other assumptions remain unchanged, but assume more rapidly decreasing costs in one industry, x say, than in the other. In this case, the horizontal axis in Fig. 2.2 becomes longer than the vertical axis. The equilibrium terms of trade will be less favourable to commodity x than the slope of the line connecting the extremities of the production frontier for both countries, since although total demand for the two commodities in the two countries taken together increases proportionately in value, because of the assumption of an equal propensity to consume each commodity, combined output of x will be larger than that of y. In this case, as in case (i), there will also be divergent gains from specialisation, arising on the supply side.

Various cases which incorporate different consumption and production conditions for each commodity can be explored in this way. It may be that on rare occasions, for example, bias on the consumption side will offset bias on the production side so that each country would be indifferent as to the activity in which it specialised completely, as in the identical economies case. But more commonly some divergence in the gains from specialisation could be expected.

Two useful generalisations emerge from the above analysis. Firstly, it is advantageous for countries to specialise completely in decreasing-cost industries for which the terms of trade are likely to become more favourable than the slope of the line connecting the extremities of the production frontier. Secondly, the more similar the propensity to consume the two commodities and the more similar the nature of scale economies in their production, the more likely it is that they can be traded with equal gain through agreed specialisation.

(iii) Finally, let all other assumptions remain unchanged, but assume that country 1 is a large country and country 2 is small. The size of a country is revealed in the size of its factor endowment, although the assumption of identical C/L ratios or factor proportions is retained. Again, inspection reveals that it is of no consequence to either country whether it specialises at one or the other extremity, M or N in Fig. 2.2. The result is the same as in the identical economies case. But the equilibrium terms of trade would become less favourable than the slope of the line connecting the extremities of the production frontier for the industry in which the large country happens to specialise production. This makes sense. Although total demand for the two commodities in both countries taken together increases proportionately in value, because of the assumption of equal propensities to consume each commodity, combined output would be larger for the commodity produced in the larger country. Thus, the gains from trade would be larger for the small country and smaller for the large country relative to their respective national incomes. Note that the terms of trade for the commodity in the production of which the large country specialises could, under certain circumstances, become so unfavourable as to induce the large country back into the production of both commodities. There would then be no gains accruing to the large country. These conclusions are quite compatible with the classical treatment of large country–small country trade.

The rationale of agreed specialisation and the conditions for its success can now be summarised. Agreed specialisation is necessary to realise economies of scale in decreasing-cost industrial activities. Countries aiming at agreement should be at the same stage of development, as measured by similarity in their factor proportions, and also be of similar size, as measured by the size of their factor endowment and the size and structure of their national markets. The more similar their production and consumption structures, the better the prospect for agreed specialisation.

Finally, what is likely to prompt countries to integrate their markets through agreed specialisation? Importantly, they will be most willing to come to some agreement on specialisation if they face competition from third countries with superior competitive power.

Introduce a third country into the model. Country 3 has a higher C/L ratio than countries 1 and 2 and larger factor endowments than either country separately, or even both of them put together. Introduce, too, a third commodity, z, the production of which requires lower capital intensity than both x and y at any factor-price ratio. Treat countries 1 and 2 as one integrated country in relation to country 3 and commodities x and y as variants of the same commodity group (say machinery) in relation to commodity z (say textiles).

If the C/L ratio is substantially lower in countries 1 and 2 than in country 3, the Heckscher–Ohlin theorem suggests that the former countries should specialise completely in the production of z and give up the production of commodities x and y. Even if the difference in the C/L ratio is not large, though they will produce all three commodities, countries 1 and 2 should remain importers of x and y and exporters of z.

In addition, assume that while commodities x and y are subject to long-run decreasing costs, z is subject to increasing costs in the long run. Then, the direction of comparative advantage already specified is even more pronounced and there will be a tendency towards complete specialisation as country 3 develops economies of scale in industries x and y where output is expanding.[31]

Countries 1 and 2 might well opt for a policy of import substitution against competition from country 3. Perhaps they attempt import substitution because of balance of payments difficulties, a faster rate of technological progress in industries x and y, a more rapid increase in demand for x and y, or because more significant external economies are expected to be created by the import-competing industries. Or perhaps, following Johnson, there is simply some 'preference for heavy industrialisation'.[32] Small market size and the low level of technology appropriate to the small market will prevent effective import competition by countries 1 and 2 separately. The only effective means of meeting country 3's superior competitive power is through agreed specialisation and regional integration. Agreed specialisation will increase industrial efficiency within the integrated markets of countries 1 and 2 and improve the position of these smaller producers against their larger competitor. It will reduce, if not eliminate, the need for inefficient protectionism.

IV. *Agreed Specialisation in Practice*

It has been argued that agreed specialisation is an essential component in regional integration which aims at the achievement of economies of scale in industrial production; that agreement will be easiest to effect between countries the greater the similarity in their structures of production and demand; and that the prime motive force towards agreed specialisation will be the superior competitive power of outside producers.

In practice, agreed specialisation might be effected through a variety of agencies: supranational planning; the reorganisation of market conditions; or rationalisation within multinational business firms.

(i) The Central American Common Market's principal objective is agreed specialisation through supranational planning among a group of small, less developed countries at a similar stage of industrialisation. 'Planned complementarity' is formally incorporated into the articles of agreement among member countries. There is provision for the joint planning and development of 'integrated industries', those industries considered to require access to the whole Common Market for efficient operation at minimum capacity. Moreover, there is provision that one such industry must be established in each participating country before a second is developed in any one member country, so that the gains from specialisation will be shared as evenly as possible. These 'integrated industries' represent agreed specialisation of the kind Sir Roy Harrod recommended to Asian developing countries.[33]

Supranational agreed specialisation seems the most appropriate course for developing countries undertaking 'a policy of regionally co-ordinated import substitution'.[34] The United Nations Conference on Trade and Development has recommended regional integration and the exchange of trade preferences among developing countries at a similar stage of industrial development in order to ensure complementarity and balance in regional development and avoid the wasteful duplication of small-scale manufacturing operations.[35] These recommendations appear to have sound justification in theory.

Supranational agreed specialisation also seems an appropriate course for centrally planned economies, which have some

68

characteristics and industrialisation objectives in common with developing countries.[36] Centrally planned economies are apparently committed to planned industrial specialisation 'on the basis of mutual co-ordination of their long-term plans, of purposeful specialisation and co-operation',[37] within the framework of the Council for Mutual Economic Assistance. But the adequacy of this particular planning mechanism is difficult for us to assess.[38]

Supranational agreed specialisation will even be appropriate within the European Economic Community as it becomes necessary to foster the development of giant industrial companies against outside competition.

(ii) Changing the institutional framework within which industrial competition takes place also provides a means towards agreed specialisation. Competitive market structures sometimes prevent the attainment of economies of scale. The development of large-scale enterprise within a unified market will often be desirable. Only mergers and specialisation agreements can foster the competitive power of industries within a newly integrated market such as the E.E.C. against outside competition from larger producers, say in the United States. It is for this reason that, subject to certain limitations, the European Economic Community favours the removal of legal and psychological barriers to mergers across national frontiers, and the conclusion of specialisation, rationalisation, joint purchasing and joint research agreements.[39] Fostering market reorganisation of this kind constitutes an important means to agreed specialisation.[40]

(iii) Rationalisation of production within multinational firms represents a final means whereby agreed specialisation may be effected. As has already been shown, the scope for agreed specialisation is greatest among producers of similar types of industrial commodities which are subject to the same production and demand conditions. Thus, agreed specialisation would commonly involve intra-industry specialisation rather than inter-industry specialisation. This has certainly been the effect of European integration.[41] Significantly, intra-industry specialisation may be made effective through the rationalisation of resources within multinational firms.[42]

The theory of agreed specialisation outlined above does not

pretend to be a comprehensive theory of economic integration. But it may be thought of as one small step towards a more comprehensive and dynamic theory of international specialisation.

It is commonly held that international trade results in unequal gains unless trading partners stand on an equal footing. Yet once countries do stand on an equal footing, traditional theory also suggests that the incentives to trade disappear. Here it has been argued that there can be significant gains from trade among similar countries through the realisation of economies of scale and dynamic comparative advantage.

In the post-Kennedy Round world, trade policies need fresh direction. The European Economic Community is still in the process of development, and free-trade schemes such as the North Atlantic Free Trade Area and the Pacific Free Trade Area are now being advocated. Regional integration has been recommended to less developed countries and is being pushed forward in Latin America. Effective regional integration is also an objective within socialist countries. In the solution of international monetary and financial problems substantial progress has been made towards international co-operation. Why not in the field of international specialisation too? The theory of agreed specialisation developed here begins to provide a foundation for such international co-operation.

3 The Proposal for a Pacific Free Trade Area

I. *Introduction*

Following the Kennedy Round of tariff reductions, international trade policies are in need of fresh direction. It is likely that Atlantic trade will undergo substantial restructuring. In the Pacific region, there is a need to develop measures for expanding trade among advanced countries (the United States, Canada, Japan, Australia and New Zealand) and trade and aid with developing countries in Asià and Latin America, in order to promote closer economic co-operation within this region. Perhaps these objectives might be best served through the establishment of a Pacific Free Trade Area.

In this chapter, we make the highly hypothetical assumption that all tariffs are removed among advanced Pacific countries, and examine the scale, character and mutual benefits for the United States, Canada, Japan, Australia and New Zealand of such a Pacific Free Trade Area.

Firstly, recent trends in Pacific trade among these five Pacific countries and their trade with developing countries in Asia and Latin America are analysed in detail. The analysis suggests that trade among the five Pacific countries has tended to become more interdependent, that there has been increased economic co-operation among these countries, and that there are some weaker trade links which can be strengthened through further trade expansion.

Secondly, the possible static effects of eliminating tariffs among five Pacific countries are estimated on the basis of 1965 trade figures. It is shown that trade expansion through the establishment of PAFTA would be more extensive than that likely to occur under the Kennedy Round. This suggests that the formation of a Pacific Free Trade Area would be an effective means of expanding trade for these five countries, especially in

71

the likelihood that another round of global tariff reductions will not be feasible within the next decade or more. The analysis also reveals how the gains from the elimination of tariffs would be distributed among the five countries and in what commodity groups trade expansion would be most significant.

Thirdly, the ways in which PAFTA members would be able to take more effective action for assisting economic development in Asian developing countries and improving access within their markets for exports from developing countries are examined.

Though this inquiry is highly hypothetical, it serves to clarify the problems and measures necessary to the promotion of regional economic development and trade growth. Steps towards freer trade and closer economic co-operation can be taken prior to the establishment of any complete Pacific Free Trade Area.

II. *A Pacific Free Trade Area*

A Pacific Free Trade Area, comprising the United States, Canada, Japan, Australia and New Zealand, seems to possess the conditions necessary for effective regional integration.

The population within the five countries is 338 million, 1·8 times as large as the European Economic Community, and gross national product was $U.S. 1,105 billion, 2·9 times as large as that of the E.E.C., in 1968. The United States is a gigantic economy, accounting for 78 per cent of the total G.N.P. within the area, and it possesses the highest income level at $U.S. 3,551 per capita. Japan's population is 101 million, half that of the United States, but her income level is the lowest, $U.S. 1,102 (although it had risen to the $U.S. 1,336 level by 1969). The income levels of Canada, Australia and New Zealand are similar, each between $U.S. 1,500 and $U.S. 2,250, and a little higher than that of the United Kingdom and the E.E.C. However, population is smaller at 20·8 million in Canada, 12·0 million in Australia and 2·8 million in New Zealand.

It is problematic whether homogeneity in the size of national economies and similarity in the stage of economic development are necessary and desirable conditions for economic integration. Since the Australia–New Zealand free-trade agreement came into force on 1 January 1966, these two countries may be well thought of as an economic unit. Thus, differences in size and per capita income can be considered as of no greater variety than those which exist among the E.E.C. or EFTA countries. But an important question which arises is whether the United States economy is so gigantic that it does not need a larger integrated market for the sake of achieving 'economies of scale'; and whether her interests, economic as well as political, are too world-wide to permit involvement in regional endeavours.

Two centres in world trade

The Pacific is one of the two major centres of world trade and ranks alongside Western Europe. Trade among the five advanced Pacific countries – the United States, Canada, Japan, Australia and New Zealand – increased by 97 per cent between 1958 and 1965, from $U.S. 9·16 billion to $U.S. 18·02 billion, and their share in world trade rose from 7·99 per cent to 10·38 per cent.

The intra-areal trade of the E.E.C. was $U.S. 6·86 billion in 1958, which was smaller than PAFTA trade, and tripled to $U.S. 20·84 billion in 1965. The share of intra-areal trade of the E.E.C. in world trade has increased from 5·98 per cent in 1958 to 12·00 per cent in 1965, more rapidly than in the case of PAFTA trade.

European trade, including E.E.C., United Kingdom and other Western European trade, increased 2·3 times from $U.S. 22·23 billion in 1958 to $U.S. 51·16 billion in 1965. Europe is one of the most important and rapidly growing centres of world trade (see Table 3.1).

With this, we can compare 'extended Pacific trade', which is the sum of the trade among countries in PAFTA, other Asia (excluding mainland China) and Latin America. Extended Pacific area trade was $U.S. 23·36 billion or 20·36 per cent of

Table 3.1. Consolidated Trade Matrix

Exports from	A PAFTA (a)	(b)	B A.L.A. (a)	(b)	C Europe (a)	(b)	Total exports (a)
A. PAFTA	9,160·5	32·45	5,457·3	19·33	7,522·0	26·65	28,226·7
	13,552·8	34·47	8,300·6	21·11	10,838·7	27·57	39,323·0
	18,021·7	37·26	9,793·5	20·25	13,474·2	27·86	48,371·0
B. Other Asia and Latin America	5,745·3	38·53	2,992·7	20·07	4,153·9	27·86	14,910·0
	6,505·5	38·17	2,194·9	12·88	5,083·7	29·84	17,040·0
	7,390·5	38·90	2,505·3	13·19	5,481·8	28·85	19,000·0
C. Europe	5,684·3	13·63	4,782·3	11·47	22,227·5	53·30	41,699·0
	7,662·3	12·02	4,956·2	7·78	40,706·8	63·87	63,739·0
	9,853·8	12·39	5,535·4	6·96	51,157·7	64·33	79,520·0
Total imports	24,299·3	21·18	16,559·8	14·44	45,885·7	40·00	114,704·3
	33,353·0	23·39	18,540·0	13·00	73,504·0	51·55	142,600·0
	41,948·0	24·15	20,660·0	11·89	90,068·0	51·85	173,700·0

Notes: (a) Value of exports in million U.S. dollars.
 (b) Areal distribution of exports (per cent).
 Upper column, 1958; middle column, 1963; lower column, 1965.
 PAFTA: United States, Canada, Japan, Australia and New Zealand.
 A.L.A.: Other Asia and Latin America. (Other Asia includes Afghanistan, Brunei, Burma, Cambodia, Ceylon, China (Taiwan), Hong Kong, India, Indonesia (incl. West Irian), Korea (South), Laos, Macao, Malayan Federation, North Borneo, Pakistan, Philippines, Ryukyus, Sarawak, Singapore, Thailand, Vietnam, British Asia n.s. (not specified), Independent Sterling Asia, Portuguese India, Portuguese Asia n.s., Asia n.s.; China and China mainland are excluded.)
 Europe: United Kingdom, E.E.C. and other Western Europe.
Source: I.M.F., *Direction of Trade*, annual 1958–62, 1961–5, a supplement to *International Financial Statistics*.

world trade in 1958, which was somewhat larger than European trade, and increased to $U.S. 37·71 billion or 21·71 per cent of world trade in 1965. Extended Pacific area trade is another centre of world trade, but it has not grown so fast as has European trade, mainly due to the stagnation in exports of primary produce from developing countries in Asia and Latin America.

The extended Pacific area could be the largest centre of world trade if there were closer co-operation in expanding trade and development within the area, since it has greater potential in the endowment of its population, natural resources and capital awaiting development than has already well-developed Europe.

Furthermore, intra-areal trade among the five Pacific countries has increased more rapidly than their trade with outside countries. The ratio of intra-areal trade for the five Pacific countries taken together increased from 32·5 per cent in 1958 to 37·3 per cent in 1965. In contrast, similar ratios for the E.E.C. were 30·1 per cent in 1958 and 43·5 per cent in 1965.

The five Pacific countries taken together increased the share of their total exports going to Asia and Latin America from 19·3 per cent in 1958 to 20·3 per cent in 1965, and that to Europe from 26·7 per cent to 27·9 per cent respectively. Thus, the effect of their trade has spread to other areas. While the share of intra-areal trade in total European trade increased from 53·3 per cent in 1958 to 64·3 per cent in 1965, the share of European trade both with the five Pacific countries and with Asia and Latin America decreased from 13·6 per cent to 12·4 per cent and from 11·5 per cent to 7·0 per cent respectively. This reflects the inward-looking trend of European trade, which, for example, has required Australia and New Zealand to turn their eyes towards the Pacific area.

In short, extended Pacific trade is one of the most important and rapidly growing centres in world trade and there is a close trade relationship between the five Pacific countries and nearby developing countries in Asia and Latin America.

PAFTA trade for each member country

The ratio of intra-areal trade for the five Pacific countries taken together, as mentioned already, increased from 32·5 per cent in 1958 to 37·3 per cent in 1965. The similar ratio for each of four of these countries also increased: from 25·2 per cent to 31·0 per cent for the United States; from 29·2 per cent to 36·8 per cent for Japan; from 27·5 per cent to 35·3 per cent for Australia; and from 22·8 per cent to 23·5 per cent for New Zealand. It decreased only for Canada from 63·0 per cent to 60·1 per cent (Table 3.2). The exceptional decrease in the Canadian ratio was due to her heavy increase of cereal exports to socialist countries.

Table 3.2. Areal Distribution of Exports
(per cent)

Exports from	a U.S.A.	b Canada	c Japan	d Australia	e N.Z.	f Pacific	g Other Asia	h Latin Am.	i U.K.	j E.E.C.	k Other W.E.	l Total exports
a. United States	–	19·14	4·71	1·06	0·24	25·16	7·73	22·75	4·68	13·56	6·76	100·00
	–	17·66	7·34	1·90	0·31	27·21	10·87	13·49	5·01	17·15	7·67	100·00
	–	20·45	7·52	2·55	0·46	30·98	7·17	13·69	5·81	18·15	10·74	100·00
b. Canada	59·45	–	2·14	1·07	0·31	62·98	2·74	3·74	15·85	8·62	2·80	100·00
	53·74	–	4·08	1·39	0·42	59·63	1·86	3·49	13·89	6·66	2·87	100·00
	54·74	–	3·44	1·56	0·40	60·14	1·67	2·92	12·85	6·89	2·75	100·00
c. Japan	24·07	2·65	–	2·18	0·26	29·16	30·49	6·73	3·66	4·31	3·39	100·00
	27·92	2·29	–	2·91	0·80	33·92	29·67	5·78	2·86	6·08	4·23	100·00
	29·78	2·54	–	3·78	0·72	36·82	25·92	4·79	2·43	5·73	4·82	100·00
d. Australia	5·81	1·79	12·33	–	7·57	27·50	9·01	0·73	29·55	18·19	2·46	100·00
	11·48	1·88	17·34	–	6·41	37·11	9·78	0·56	17·98	14·50	2·70	100·00
	10·99	1·40	16·63	–	6·32	35·34	10·61	0·98	17·62	14·44	3·11	100·00
e. New Zealand	14·87	1·63	2·20	4·11	–	22·81	0·90	0·17	55·63	14·15	1·06	100·00
	17·24	1·38	4·86	5·22	–	28·70	1·80	0·26	45·45	16·87	0·67	100·00
	12·36	1·37	5·13	4·65	–	23·52	1·67	0·41	48·11	15·50	1·02	100·00
f. Pacific countries	13·87	12·56	4·16	1·19	0·68	32·45	9·06	15·84	9·32	12·02	5·31	100·00
	14·35	10·99	6·41	1·90	0·82	34·47	11·63	9·47	8·10	13·61	5·85	100·00
	15·80	12·14	6·00	2·48	0·85	37·26	11·07	9·17	8·07	13·71	6·08	100·00
g. Other Asia	14·40	1·17	8·11	3·42	0·57	27·67	31·18	1·80	14·17	10·39	2·35	100·00
	15·13	1·50	12·38	1·80	0·58	31·39	16·53	1·18	11·37	9·72	3·11	100·00
	17·37	1·63	12·85	2·06	0·85	34·49	15·61	1·02	9·85	9·63	3·12	100·00
h. Latin America	44·07	1·42	1·98	0·05	0·01	47·53	0·34	9·04	8·26	15·40	4·98	100·00
	36·40	3·32	4·01	0·12	0·12	43·97	0·70	8·06	7·68	21·23	5·74	100·00
	34·78	3·48	4·15	0·10	0·03	42·54	0·56	9·77	6·33	20·81	6·90	100·00
i. United Kingdom	8·82	5·77	0·60	7·08	3·84	26·11	11·09	4·55	–	13·79	17·85	100·00
	8·57	4·24	1·20	5·62	2·74	22·37	9·52	3·35	–	21·08	20·66	100·00
	10·61	4·25	1·08	5·78	2·57	24·30	8·26	2·99	–	20·02	21·36	100·00
j. E.E.C.	7·33	1·04	0·61	0·75	0·20	9·92	4·74	6·56	5·84	30·14	21·00	100·00
	6·83	0·82	0·95	0·65	0·14	9·41	3·01	3·93	5·26	42·43	21·18	100·00
	7·15	1·00	0·71	0·69	0·13	9·68	3·02	3·35	4·94	43·48	21·03	100·00
k. Other W. Europe	7·91	0·82	0·50	0·80	0·16	10·19	2·14	5·62	16·79	32·35	16·74	100·00
	7·74	0·84	0·78	0·79	0·17	10·32	2·22	3·52	15·53	33·53	19·99	100·00
	7·83	0·93	0·79	0·84	0·14	10·53	2·16	3·10	14·93	31·64	21·62	100·00
l. Total imports	11·69	4·67	2·64	1·57	0·62	21·18	7·31	7·12	9·21	20·05	10·74	100·00
	12·07	4·28	4·72	1·74	0·58	23·39	7·52	5·48	9·45	28·34	13·75	100·00
	12·34	4·61	4·70	1·94	0·56	24·15	6·91	4·99	9·29	28·21	14·35	100·00

Note: Upper column, 1958; middle column, 1963; lower column, 1965.

Source: *Direction of Trade*, annual 1958–62, 1961–5, a supplement to *International Financial Statistics*.

The importance of exports to Europe increased for the United States from 25 per cent in 1958 to 33 per cent in 1965 and for Japan from 11 per cent to 13 per cent, while it decreased for Australia from 50 per cent to 35 per cent, for Canada from 27 per cent to 22 per cent, and for New Zealand from 70 per cent to 65 per cent. Thus, we clearly see the growing importance of the Pacific trade for the five countries which together provided new trade outlets for the three British Commonwealth partners.

Taking the total exports (equals imports) of PAFTA trade as 100, the composition of intra-areal trade is shown in Fig. 3.1. The share of Japan's exports in PAFTA trade showed the most

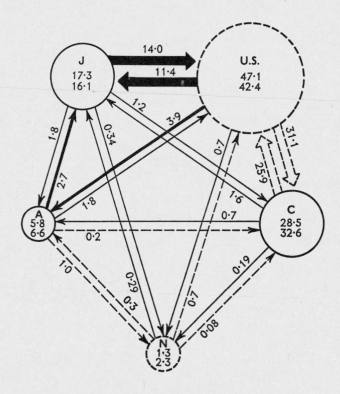

Figure 3.1: Share in the total intra-areal trade of five Pacific countries: total trade of each country in 1965 (per cent).

Note: (1) Figures in the circle show the share of each country's exports (upper figure) to and imports (lower figure) from the Pacific countries.
(2) Figures along the line show the share of each bilateral trade.
(3) Solid line and circle show the increase of importance, dotted ones the decrease of importance during the period 1958-65.

Source: *Direction of Trade*, annual 1958-62, 1961-5, a supplement to *International Financial Statistics*.

77

rapid rate of increase, rising from 9·2 per cent in 1958 to 17·3 per cent in 1965, and that of Australia also increased from 5·0 per cent to 5·8 per cent, while the similar share decreased for the United States from 49·2 per cent to 47·1 per cent, for Canada from 34·9 per cent to 28·5 per cent, and for New Zealand from 1·7 per cent to 1·3 per cent. The decrease in the American share was mainly due to the relative decrease of exports to Canada. The share of American exports to the other three countries increased. It is clear that Japan, Australia and the United States were growth centres in the expansion of PAFTA trade, while Canada and New Zealand have been weaker links. The share in the total PAFTA trade of Japanese imports and exports to each of the PAFTA countries, without exception, increased. A similar trend can be seen in American and Australian trade with PAFTA countries other than Canada and New Zealand.

The importance of the PAFTA market for each member country varies (see Table 3.2). Owing to special dependence upon the United States market, Canadian exports destined to the Pacific area were as high as 60·1 per cent in 1965, but if the United States market is excluded, the United Kingdom market was more important for Canada than the Japanese, Australian and New Zealand markets. The United States exported 31 per cent of her total exports to the Pacific area, which was as important as the Western European (United Kingdom, E.E.C. and other Western Europe) market. One-third of the exports from Japan and Australia went to the Pacific area. The most important market for Japan was the United States, while it was Japan for Australia as far as the Pacific area was concerned. Australia and New Zealand until recently were more interested in markets in the United Kingdom and E.E.C. countries, but especially since the emergence of the E.E.C. and negotiations on Britain's entry into it, the eyes of Australia and New Zealand have been increasingly turning away from Britain, towards the Pacific area and towards Asian developing countries.

Japan's interest in trade with Asian developing countries is greatest among the five Pacific countries. Exports to Asia ('Other Asia' in the tables) accounted for 26 per cent of Japan's total exports in 1965. However, Australia as well as the United States also have a substantial interest in Asian developing-

78

country trade. The five Pacific countries taken together exported 11·1 per cent of their total exports to Asian developing countries. The only country outside the Pacific which is equally interested in trade with Asian developing countries is the United Kingdom.[1] Moreover, in 1965 the five Pacific countries took 15·6 per cent of Asian exports. These close trade relations between advanced Pacific countries and Asian developing countries require special consideration. They suggest that the formation of a Pacific Free Trade Area might be beneficially

Table 3.3. Intensity of Trade

Exports from	to	a. U.S.A.	b. Canada	c. Japan	d. Australia	e. N.Z.	f. Pacific	g. Other Asia	h. Latin Am.	i. U.K.	j. E.E.C.	k. Other W.E.
a. United States		–	362	158	60	34	168	125	310	45	85	64
		–	363	137	96	47	172	144	239	47	88	57
		–	389	140	115	72	197	102	273	55	98	78
b. Canada		485	–	77	65	48	455	48	55	164	58	29
		426	–	83	76	69	411	27	67	141	37	23
		423	–	70	77	68	417	26	63	132	41	22
c. Japan		200	55	–	129	41	215	542	101	39	30	35
		220	51	–	159	131	233	427	111	29	34	34
		230	52	–	185	122	255	402	104	25	34	38
d. Australia		49	38	460	–	1,202	205	162	11	316	127	26
		93	43	361	–	1,086	263	145	11	187	83	23
		87	30	347	–	1,109	252	169	22	186	87	25
e. New Zealand		126	35	83	260	–	172	16	3	600	100	11
		142	32	102	298	–	206	27	5	478	98	6
		100	30	109	238	–	170	27	9	515	95	8
f. Pacific countries		103	233	137	66	96	213	144	212	88	74	49
		102	221	117	94	122	214	151	164	74	68	43
		110	227	113	110	146	233	155	180	75	73	43
g. Other Asia		116	24	291	206	86	198	538	18	145	70	24
		117	33	245	97	94	211	233	22	112	53	25
		132	33	256	100	97	235	239	22	100	56	24
h. Latin America		353	28	70	3	2	337	6	130	84	102	50
		287	74	81	7	20	301	10	154	77	118	46
		269	72	84	5	5	295	9	212	65	123	54
i. United Kingdom		69	112	21	409	565	180	184	64	–	89	173
		64	90	23	293	428	146	130	61	–	111	159
		78	84	21	270	415	160	122	62	–	112	160
j. E.E.C.		54	19	20	41	28	65	74	87	54	184	193
		47	16	17	31	20	56	38	66	46	205	149
		49	18	13	30	19	59	41	64	45	224	145
k. Other Western Europe		61	16	17	46	24	70	35	79	165	208	162
		57	17	15	40	26	66	30	63	145	172	150
		56	18	15	38	22	67	31	62	141	171	175

Note: Upper column, 1958; middle column, 1963; lower column, 1965.
Source: Calculated from Table 3.2.

accompanied by the extension of associate membership for nearby developing countries.[2]

These close trade relations can be shown more exactly by the intensity of trade indices[3] (see Table 3.3). The intensity of intra-areal trade, exports and imports, of each member country within the Pacific region was more than 100 in 1965. Five Pacific countries traded with each other intensively. In exports, the order of intensity was 417 for Canada, 255 for Japan, 252 for Australia, 197 for the United States and 170 for New Zealand.

United States–Canada trade was very intensive (389 and 423) and Australia–New Zealand trade was also intensive, although there was a big imbalance in the indices of 1,109 for Australian exports and 238 for New Zealand's exports. These high intensities are naturally due to the special geographical and institutional proximity of these two countries. Japan traded intensively with the United States (230 and 140) and Australia (185 and 347). High intensities derive mainly from complementary trade in manufactures and primary products. It is interesting to find that the United States' trade with Western Europe was far less intensive than her trade with Pacific countries.

As compared with these four intensive bilateral trade relations, the other six bilateral trade relations (i.e. New Zealand–United States, New Zealand–Canada, New Zealand–Japan, Canada–Australia, Canada–Japan and Australia–United States) were less intensive. With the exception of Japan, the four countries are competitive with each other as exporters of primary products, and Canada, Australia and New Zealand have in the past looked towards the United Kingdom and/or the E.E.C. for markets for their primary products and for supplies of imported manufactured commodities.

Trade relations with Asian developing countries were also intensive for advanced Pacific countries taken together (155 for their exports and 235 for Asian exports). Japan had the most intensive trade relations with Asian developing countries (402 and 256), higher than Australia (169 and 100) and the United States (102 and 132). However, trade intensities of Canada and New Zealand with Asian developing countries were very low.

80

In order to carry out a commodity analysis of PAFTA trade, trade matrices of eight commodity groups were calculated from United Nations *Commodity Trade Statistics* for 1958 and 1965. The commodity groups are:[4]

N_1 goods: staple foods (rice, wheat and other grains).

N_2 goods: other foodstuffs, including processed goods.

N_3 goods: agricultural raw materials.

N_4 goods: minerals, metals and fuels.

L_1 goods: labour-intensive goods of light industry, both intermediate and final products.

L_2 goods: labour-intensive final goods of heavy and chemical industry origin (cameras, sewing machines, bicycles, precision-type equipment, medicine, etc.).

K_1 goods: capital-intensive intermediate goods of heavy and chemical industry origin (pig-iron, steel, chemical fibres, fertiliser, etc.).

K_2 goods: capital-intensive heavy machines and equipment.

Further, N_1 and N_2 goods are aggregated as Food (F), N_3 and N_4 goods as Raw Materials (R), L_1 and L_2 goods as Light Manufactures (L), and K_1 and K_2 goods as Heavy Manufactures and Chemicals (K), for the convenience of analysis.

In order to consider how to expand trade among the five advanced Pacific countries as well as their trade with Asian developing countries, we face two important problems.

First, the four countries in the Pacific economic community, other than Japan, appear competitive not only with each other but also with Asian developing countries in exporting agricultural products and some natural-resource-intensive goods. Intra-areal trade in those commodities within the Pacific region would increase if they reduced or abolished tariffs and other trade restrictions through the establishment of a Pacific Free Trade Area. In order to provide Asian developing countries with a much wider opportunity for exporting primary products, it would be necessary for advanced Pacific countries to increase assistance for developing primary production in

Asian countries and to undertake the structural adjustments necessary for providing them with larger markets.

Secondly, a similar problem is seen for expanding trade in manufactured goods. Here, the liberalisation of trade through PAFTA would work most effectively. At the same time, the Pacific countries should open up their markets for light manufactures produced by Asian developing countries in exchange for the former's capital goods.

The composition of PAFTA trade for each country exhibits different characteristics. In Japanese trade with PAFTA countries in 1965, 94·8 per cent of exports were manufactures while 71·1 per cent of imports were primary products. Japan's trade is mainly of the vertical type, specialising in exports of manufactured goods. Australia and New Zealand maintain another type of vertical trade, specialising in exports of primary products: 80·0 per cent of exports were primary commodities in the case of Australia and 82·4 per cent in the case of New Zealand, while imports were 88·2 per cent and 84·6 per cent in manufactured goods respectively. The United States and Canada maintain a balance in the trade of manufactures as well as primary products between exports and imports: manufactured goods occupy 70·0 per cent both in exports and

Table 3.4. PAFTA Trade by Commodity in 1965
Relative to 1958

(1958 = 100)

N_1	235·5
N_2	160·6
N_3	183·5
N_4	163·8
L_1	186·3
L_2	252·4
K_1	232·4
K_2	288·9
F	180·7
R	173·4
L	199·6
K	263·8

Source: Based on data and commodity classification described in the text.

imports for the United States and 60·5 per cent and 79·6 per cent in exports and imports respectively for Canada. It is to be expected, therefore, that the two countries should conduct horizontal-type trade with the PAFTA countries.

Relative to the growth of total PAFTA trade from 100 in 1958 to 197 in 1965, trade in heavy manufactures and chemicals (K goods) has grown fastest (264), followed by trade in light manufactures (200) in which, however, the more sophisticated goods (L_2 goods) have grown almost as fast as K goods (252), while trade in food and raw materials has grown at a slower rate than total trade (181 and 173 respectively) (see Table 3.4). Heavy manufactures and chemicals as well as sophisticated labour-intensive goods have been the leading sectors in PAFTA

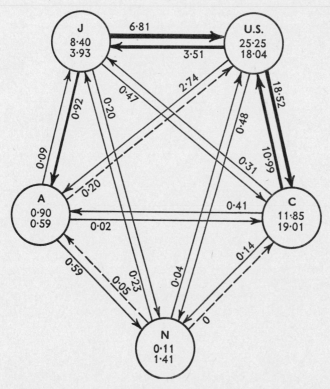

Figure 3.2: Share in the total intra-areal trade of five Pacific countries: heavy manufactures and chemicals (K goods). Total share, 46·51 per cent.

Note: See Fig. 3.1.

trade, with food, raw materials and traditional light manufactures (L_1 goods) the lagging sectors.

Fig. 3.2 clearly shows that the importance of bilateral trade in K goods (the total share in PAFTA trade was as large as 46·5 per cent in 1965) has rapidly increased in almost all directions except in three unimportant cases, i.e. Australia–United States, New Zealand–Australia and New Zealand–Canada. The United States and Japan are in export surplus while Canada, Australia and New Zealand are in import surplus. In L goods (the total share was 20·6 per cent), except in only one case (Canada–United States), the importance of bilateral trade has also increased in all directions (Fig. 3.3). Only Japan is in heavy

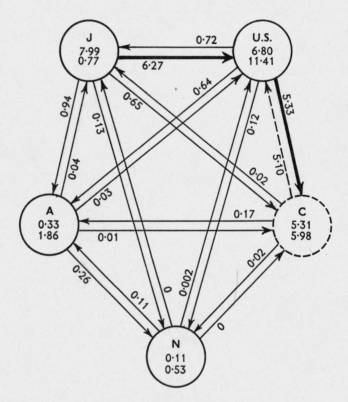

Figure 3.3: Share in the total intra-areal trade of five Pacific countries: light manufactures (L goods). Total share, 20·55 per cent.

Note: See Fig. 3.1.

export surplus while the other four countries are in import surplus.

Raw materials are as important as *L* goods in PAFTA trade, the total share being 20·5 per cent (Fig. 3.4). The United States and Japan are net importing countries while Canada, Australia and New Zealand are net exporting countries. The most

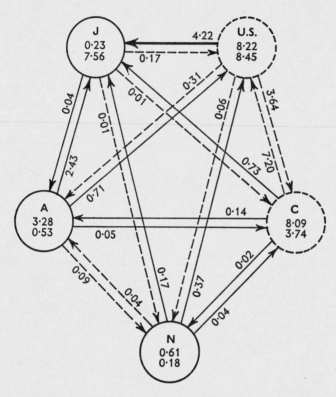

Figure 3.4: Share in the total intra-areal trade of five Pacific countries: raw materials (*R* goods). Total share, 20·45 per cent.
Note: See Fig. 3.1.

significant change during the period 1958–65 was the increase in importance of Australian exports to Japan, the United States and Canada and the decrease in bilateral trade between the United States and Canada.

Food is the least important commodity category (11·3 per

cent) in PAFTA trade, and only Japan is a net importer (Fig. 3.5). The most significant change was the decrease in importance of trade between America and Canada.

The expansion of horizontal trade in manufactured goods can be regarded as the primary accelerator of rapid growth and

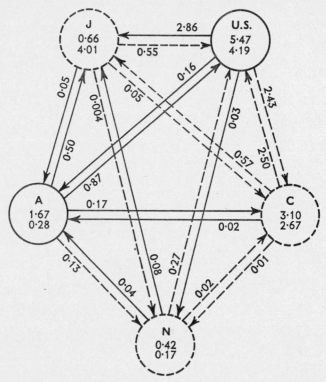

Figure 3.5: Share in the total intra-areal trade of five Pacific countries:
food (*F* goods). Total share, 11·32 per cent.
Note: See Fig. 3.1.

prosperity of the E.E.C.'s intra-bloc trade.[5] In order to ascertain whether or not similar progress in horizontal trade between the PAFTA countries has been taking place, the degree of horizontal trade[6] was calculated (Table 3.5).

(i) The aggregate degree of horizontal trade within PAFTA for all commodities, $\bar{D}_T$, in 1965, was high in the case of the United States and Canada, 54·8 and 50·3 respectively, while

86

Table 3.5. Degree of Horizontal Trade in Pacific Countries

| | (a) Trade between each two countries ||||||||| | (b) Trade of each country with PAFTA |||||
	a·b	d·e	a·c	b·c	a·d	b·d	b·e	a·e	c·e	c·d	a·f	b·f	c·f	d·f	e·f
D·N₁	46·7 / 17·5	0·4 / 1·1	0·2 / 0·2	0·04 / 0	0 / 0	0 / 0	0 / 0	0 / 0	0 / 0	0 / 0	41·3 / 50·2	20·5 / 82·5	0·1 / 0·1	0·2 / 1·2	0·4 / 1·1
N₂	58·6 / 68·2	50·6 / 66·3	17·6 / 74·3	34·7 / 62·9	12·9 / 17·9	11·1 / 13·1	11·7 / 29·0	2·5 / 10·7	94·3 / 4·5	43·9 / 19·5	44·2 / 62·4	64·2 / 76·6	18·9 / 58·9	28·6 / 19·9	14·2 / 24·6
N₃	45·2 / 57·8	74·6 / 98·7	7·5 / 5·8	8·9 / 3·1	82·5 / 28·0	38·2 / 57·1	58·9 / 28·3	5·3 / 6·8	5·9 / 0·9	0·3 / 1·1	97·2 / 88·3	44·4 / 53·9	4·8 / 3·8	20·5 / 12·8	17·3 / 12·1
N₄	48·3 / 46·0	0·7 / 1·6	0·1 / 1·4	0 / 0·2	96·2 / 84·0	0 / 6·5	0 / 0	0 / 0	0 / 84·3	0·9 / 3·2	66·8 / 84·1	47·1 / 41·3	0·1 / 1·8	33·6 / 23·7	7·8 / 4·9
L₁	34·1 / 62·7	64·7 / 97·3	2·5 / 7·6	0·3 / 2·2	24·5 / 7·5	3·0 / 1·3	0 / 0	4·1 / 0·2	0·2 / 0·3	2·2 / 4·4	24·2 / 39·7	39·9 / 71·1	2·2 / 6·6	21·7 / 11·3	33·9 / 32·9
L₂	8·9 / 15·8	1·0 / 2·5	33·5 / 24·9	5·6 / 0·4	2·9 / 0·2	0 / 23·8	0 / 0	0 / 0	0 / 0	0·1 / 0·1	36·1 / 59·6	9·5 / 16·3	28·8 / 21·2	17·0 / 43·7	0·3 / 1·8
K₁	26·7 / 63·7	18·3 / 12·2	68·7 / 32·7	80·3 / 94·1	95·8 / 33·5	1·4 / 9·9	6·8 / 0	48·7 / 40·0	39·9 / 15·5	29·8 / 19·5	84·2 / 57·4	73·4 / 63·1	75·2 / 35·0	80·7 / 53·2	24·8 / 15·8
K₂	18·4 / 31·2	2·0 / 3·6	31·9 / 73·6	18·3 / 14·2	2·1 / 0·5	1·4 / 1·7	0 / 0	0·3 / 0·2	0 / 0	7·4 / 0·8	19·0 / 39·6	19·9 / 33·2	39·5 / 60·8	17·3 / 9·5	1·0 / 1·3
D:T	43·6 / 47·2	26·3 / 30·5	18·2 / 30·2	7·8 / 21·9	48·2 / 16·1	10·2 / 13·1	12·6 / 9·0	5·9 / 8·4	15·4 / 6·5	2·6 / 5·2	53·3 / 54·8	44·3 / 50·3	17·1 / 24·1	30·1 / 20·4	15·4 / 13·8
F	57·1 / 58·4	21·2 / 40·7	7·7 / 28·2	3·6 / 9·5	12·9 / 17·4	11·4 / 13·0	11·7 / 29·0	2·5 / 10·7	94·3 / 4·5	10·8 / 11·3	43·6 / 58·5	55·5 / 78·1	6·9 / 22·5	17·5 / 16·9	12·1 / 21·8
R	47·1 / 50·7	27·8 / 56·0	5·4 / 4·1	4·8 / 1·3	87·2 / 42·4	29·0 / 39·5	49·3 / 24·3	4·7 / 6·2	5·0 / 4·7	0·4 / 1·8	84·4 / 86·2	46·1 / 46·4	3·7 / 3·1	23·9 / 16·2	14·2 / 11·1
N	50·5 / 53·1	24·9 / 47·2	6·2 / 14·6	3·8 / 5·1	69·3 / 29·7	22·4 / 26·2	22·0 / 25·9	3·3 / 8·0	18·8 / 4·7	1·5 / 3·5	70·3 / 76·0	49·5 / 56·8	4·8 / 10·3	22·5 / 16·4	13·1 / 15·7
L	29·0 / 50·4	58·9 / 55·1	8·3 / 12·0	1·4 / 1·8	13·1 / 4·9	2·8 / 5·1	0 / 0	1·9 / 0·1	8·5 / 0·3	2·1 / 3·9	26·7 / 44·9	33·8 / 56·9	7·3 / 10·0	21·0 / 19·5	27·7 / 22·1
K	22·4 / 44·9	13·6 / 8·6	21·5 / 54·2	43·2 / 69·1	36·7 / 9·0	1·4 / 4·9	2·2 / 0	18·6 / 10·9	30·8 / 12·3	23·0 / 11·2	52·0 / 46·3	44·9 / 44·3	54·1 / 48·0	47·7 / 25·2	14·8 / 8·6
L+K	39·6 / 44·9	27·· / 25·3	26· / 43·5	12·9 / 38·0	33·7 / 8·2	1·9 / 4·9	2·0 / 0	14·4 / 8·8	8·5 / 7·8	5·9 / 7·8	42·9 / 45·9	41·2 / 47·7	27·3 / 32·2	39·1 / 23·5	18·9 / 12·6

Note: a = United States, b = Canada, c = Japan, d = Australia, e = New Zealand, f = PAFTA. Upper column, 1958; lower column, 1965.

Source: Based on data and methods described in the text.

that of Japan (24·1), Australia (20·4) and New Zealand (13·8) was low. In bilateral trade, $\overline{D}_T$ was high only in the American–Canadian trade (47·2) and low in all other cases, ranging from 30·5 to 5·2. The higher figures compare well with intra-areal trade in the E.E.C. which, however, has no lower degree even in bilateral trade.

(ii) In the E.E.C., the degree of horizontal trade increased rapidly in general from 1956–8 to 1965. In PAFTA trade, the degree has increased from 1958 to 1965 in bilateral trade among the United States, Canada and Japan, while it has decreased in Australia–PAFTA, Australia–America, New Zealand–PAFTA, New Zealand–Canada and New Zealand–Japan trade.

(iii) Higher figures for horizontal trade by commodity (D), and/or those which show the most significant increase, are to be found in heavy manufactures and chemicals (K_1 and K_2) among the trade of the United States, Canada and Japan; for example, in K goods it has increased from 22 in 1958 to 43 in 1965 in American–Canadian trade, from 22 to 54 in American–Japanese trade, and from 43 to 69 in Canadian–Japanese trade. These higher degrees of horizontal trade in heavy manufactures and chemicals are equivalent to those in the E.E.C. The trade of Australia and New Zealand in this commodity category is low and the degree of horizontal trade with other PAFTA countries in it is decreasing.

(iv) Higher degrees of horizontal trade in raw materials (R goods) are shown in the trade of America–Canada, America–Australia, Canada–Australia, Canada–New Zealand and Australia–New Zealand. The promotion of horizontal trade in raw materials between the PAFTA countries, except Japan, would be fruitful. In food (F goods), horizontal trade has not progressed except in the trade of America–Canada and Australia–New Zealand.

In short, horizontal trade between PAFTA countries, with the exception of American–Canadian trade, is not well developed relative to that of the E.E.C. This would suggest that there is plenty of room to expand PAFTA trade through the promotion of horizontal trade, particularly in heavy manufactures and chemicals, but also in raw materials as well.

Summary

The analysis of recent trends in Pacific trade reveals that trade between the five Pacific countries (United States, Canada, Japan, Australia and New Zealand) has been growing rapidly, and that interdependence has intensified. This provides a foundation for moving towards closer economic co-operation and, perhaps, towards economic integration.

Secondly, although extended Pacific trade had achieved the same scale as European trade in 1958, the latter grew more rapidly than the former thereafter. This suggests a need for closer economic co-operation in the extended Pacific region which possesses huge potential for economic development.

Thirdly, the growth centres of PAFTA trade have been Japan, Australia and the United States, while Canada and New Zealand have been lagging behind. Heavy manufactures and chemicals, as well as sophisticated light manufactures, have been leading sectors in trade expansion, while trade in primary produce and traditional light manufactures has been relatively stagnant. Differences by commodity in the growth of trade bear a close relation to the growth rate of each country's trade.

These trends suggest the main policy targets for further expansion of Pacific trade.

III. *Static Effects of PAFTA*

The formation of a Pacific Free Trade Area would, in fact, bring about more comprehensive trade liberalisation among participating countries, with the elimination of tariffs on a substantial proportion of their commodity trade, and would result in a larger trade expansion than is possible through tariff reductions of the Kennedy Round type. Complete regional trade liberalisation would appear to have considerable advantages over partial trade liberalisation in world markets. This is especially true if, as is most probable, another major round of global tariff reductions is not feasible within the next decade or more. In that event, the formation of PAFTA would seem an

89

effective alternative for mutual trade expansion among the five advanced Pacific countries.

Effects of tariff elimination in PAFTA

Here an attempt is made to estimate the impact of the elimination of tariffs upon the five Pacific countries which might constitute a Pacific Free Trade Area, on the basis of 1965 trade figures. The method of the estimation is the same as that used in Chapter 1, section III.

All commodities which accounted for $U.S. 10 million or more of each country's imports in 1965 are taken into consideration. The coverage is about 90 per cent for each country. Tariff data are derived from two publications, from P.E.P.'s *Tariffs and Trade in Western Europe* and *Atlantic Tariffs and Trade*, and the Customs Tariffs of Japan, Australia and New Zealand.

The impact effect of Pacific tariff elimination would be to increase trade by $U.S. 5,000 million. This represents an expansion of 28 per cent on intra-areal trade, or 10·3 per cent on Pacific country exports to, and 11·9 per cent on imports from, the whole world. In other words, there would be significant trade expansion (Table 3.6).[7]

The gains from tariff elimination would not be equally distributed among the five Pacific countries involved. Japan's exports would increase by $U.S. 1,740 million, or 56 per cent on her total exports to PAFTA countries, and her imports would increase by $U.S. 430 million, or 14·7 per cent on her total imports from PAFTA countries. Japan's trade balance with the Pacific, which was roughly in equilibrium in 1965, would consequently improve by $U.S. 1,310 million. United States exports would increase by $U.S. 2,300 million, or 27·9 per cent, and imports by $U.S. 2,280 million, or 30·1 per cent, and the favourable balance in United States trade with the Pacific, of about $U.S. 850 million in 1965, would be preserved. On the other hand, imports would rise more rapidly than exports for the remaining three countries. Canada's exports would increase by $U.S. 855 million but her imports would rise by $U.S. 1,480 million; Australia's exports would increase by $U.S. 65 million, whereas her imports would rise by $U.S. 650

million; and New Zealand's exports would grow by $U.S. 22 million, while her imports would rise by $U.S. 140 million.

The differential pattern of gains depends principally upon whether the country's exports are more or less heavily concentrated in manufactures, and suggests a need for fostering further industrialisation in Canada, Australia and New Zealand. Indeed, the pursuit of this objective would be facilitated through the dynamic effects of establishing a larger and completely free regional market, and through the freer movement of capital, technical know-how and managerial skills among member countries. The most important fact to be noted, how-

Table 3.6. Static Effects of the Formation of PAFTA

(a) Value of increase (million U.S. dollars)   (base year = 1965)

		a U.S.A.	b Canada	c Japan	d Australia	e N.Z.	Pacific countries
a. United States	ΔX	–	1,404·6	404·4	426·3	66·4	2,301·7
	ΔM	–	791·5	1,457·5	23·6	10·5	2,283·2
	$\Delta X - \Delta M$	–	613·1	–1,053·1	402·7	55·9	18·5
b. Canada	ΔX	791·5	–	17·2	39·5	7·2	855·4
	ΔM	1,404·6	–	75·9	0·2	0·1	1,480·8
	$\Delta X - \Delta M$	–613·1	–	–58·7	39·3	7·1	–625·4
c. Japan	ΔX	1,457·5	75·9	–	176·7	33·0	1,743·1
	ΔM	404·4	17·2	–	7·6	3·5	430·7
	$\Delta X - \Delta M$	1,053·1	58·7	–	169·1	29·5	1,312·4
d. Australia	ΔX	23·6	0·2	7·6	–	33·2	64·5
	ΔM	426·3	39·5	216·2	–	8·1	650·6
	$\Delta X - \Delta M$	–402·7	–39·3	–208·6	–	25·1	–586·1
e. New Zealand	ΔX	10·5	0·1	3·4	8·1	–	22·1
	ΔM	66·4	7·2	33·0	33·2	–	139·7
	$\Delta X - \Delta M$	–55·9	–7·1	–29·6	–25·1	–	–117·6
Pacific countries	ΔX						4,986·8
	X						18,021·7

(b) Rate of increase (per cent) in trade due to the elimination of tariffs

		a U.S.A.	b Canada	c Japan	d Australia	e N.Z.	Pacific countries
a. United States	$\Delta X/X$	–	26·06	19·85	61·48	53·13	27·92
	$\Delta M/M$	–	17·03	58·59	7·24	8·56	30·10
b. Canada	$\Delta X/X$	17·03	–	5·86	29·79	20·95	16·74
	$\Delta M/M$	26·06	–	35·43	0·44	0·94	26·17
c. Japan	$\Delta X/X$	58·59	35·43	–	50·25	54·17	55·97
	$\Delta M/M$	19·85	5·86	–	1·37	7·02	14·69
d. Australia	$\Delta X/X$	7·24	0·44	1·37	–	17·13	5·79
	$\Delta M/M$	61·48	29·79	61·48	–	18·95	53·32
e. New Zealand	$\Delta X/X$	8·56	0·94	6·85	18·95	–	9·76
	$\Delta M/M$	53·14	20·95	54·17	17·13	–	33·77
Pacific countries	$\Delta X/X$						27·67

Source: Based on data and methods described in the text.

ever, is that the expansion of intra-areal trade would be larger if the five countries could effect tariff elimination.[8]

As shown in Table 3.7, in terms of intra-areal trade in 1965, the increase of trade in food and raw materials would be limited (4·5 per cent and 2·0 per cent respectively) while that of light manufactures as well as heavy manufactures and

Table 3.7. Static Effects of PAFTA: By Commodity Groups

		Food		Raw materials		Light manufactures		Heavy mnfs and chemicals	
		ΔX or ΔM	ΔX/X or ΔM/M	ΔX or ΔM	ΔX/X or ΔM/M	ΔX or ΔM	ΔX/X or ΔM/M	ΔX or ΔM	ΔX/X or ΔM/M
a. United	Ex.	34·4$m.	3·49%	27·9$m.	1·88%	432·0$m.	35·22%	1,807·4$m.	39·73%
States	Im.	43·4	5·75	38·9	2·55	933·5	45·40	1,267·4	38·98
	Bal.	−9·0		−11·0		−501·5		540·0	
b. Canada	Ex.	18·6	3·33	27·7	1·90	177·3	18·52	631·8	29·60
	Im.	6·4	1·33	12·9	1·92	332·0	30·79	1,129·4	32·97
	Bal.	12·2		14·8		−154·7		−497·6	
c. Japan	Ex.	29·9	25·07	1·6	3·96	888·2	61·68	823·3	54·40
	Im.	23·5	3·25	8·8	0·65	79·8	11·54	318·6	44·96
	Bal.	6·4		−7·2		808·4		504·7	
d. Australia	Ex.	6·7	2·24	11·8	1·99	8·8	14·56	37·2	22·89
	Im.	11·3	22·77	9·2	9·72	138·1	41·31	491·9	66·35
	Bal.	−4·6		2·6		−129·3		−454·7	
e. New Zealand	Ex.	1·2	1·59	4·9	4·45	4·3	22·17	11·7	56·95
	Im.	6·3	19·94	4·1	12·65	25·2	26·18	104·2	41·03
	Bal.	−5·1		0·8		−20·9		−92·5	
Pacific countries	Ex.	90·8	4·45	73·9	2·01	1,510·6	40·79	3,311·4	39·51
Total exports of Pacific countries in 1965		2,040·3		3,684·6		3,703·5		8,381·1	

Source: Based on data and methods described in the text.

chemicals would be considerable (40·8 per cent and 39·5 per cent respectively). This is also true for each country. These results are as might be expected, since existing tariffs and elasticities of demand are low for primary products and high for manufactures. Thus, the elimination of tariffs would promote trade in manufactures of the area as a whole and bilateral horizontal trade, but it would not stimulate, to the same degree, trade in primary products. These differences result from a variety of effects in each country along the lines mentioned above.

Table 3.7 also shows how the trade balance between each pair of countries would change. Japan would improve her trade balance with all four countries in the area; the United States

92

would do the same with three countries, except Japan; Canada's trade balance would deteriorate with the United States and Japan, while improving with Australia and New Zealand; Australia's would deteriorate with the three countries other than New Zealand; and New Zealand's would deteriorate with all four countries. These results, as already mentioned, depend upon the degree of concentration of exports in manufactures or in primary products respectively.

In view of close trade ties and greater possibilities for increasing trade through the reduction or elimination of tariffs, a Pacific Free Trade Area among the United States, Canada, Japan, Australia and New Zealand is an objective worth study, although there are a number of problems which need to be solved before its establishment.

The estimation of the effects of trade liberalisation makes some of these problems clear:

(i) Although the establishment of PAFTA would result in a sizeable expansion of intra-areal trade as a whole, the distribution of gains between the exporting and the importing countries of manufactured goods would be so unequal that no consensus towards the establishment of PAFTA would be obtainable. Before its establishment, concerted action by the PAFTA countries to promote export-oriented industrialisation in Canada, Australia and New Zealand would be necessary.

(ii) As shown in Table 3.7, heavy manufactures and chemicals would expand remarkably owing to the elimination of tariffs both in exports and imports in all the five Pacific countries. The promotion of horizontal trade within the area in these commodities should be the primary goal sought by the five countries whether through the establishment of PAFTA or through alternative measures. These industries can realise the largest dynamic effects through the enlargement of markets and through the freer movement of capital and technical and managerial know-how beyond national frontiers. These dynamic effects would work more favourably for the relatively small countries which have abundant natural resources. It should be noted that the freer movement of capital in this area is much needed in order to promote horizontal trade in heavy manufactures and chemicals.

(iii) It is estimated that trade in raw materials will expand

93

by a very small percentage (2·0 per cent in PAFTA as a whole), but greater potential for expansion of this trade can be expected, particularly in the exports of mineral products from Australia and Canada. Further expansion of heavy and chemical industries in the Pacific region would require a rapid development of trade in raw materials and intermediate goods within the area. The import surplus of Canada, Australia and New Zealand in heavy manufactures and chemicals would be covered by the export surplus from them in raw materials. In agricultural raw materials, however, room for exporting should be provided to developing countries in so far as they can produce them competitively.

(iv) In trade in light manufactures, the rate of increase due to liberalisation would also be large (40·8 per cent in PAFTA as a whole), but only Japan would enjoy a net increase in exports. Requests for protection of these light manufacturing industries in the United States, Canada, Australia and New Zealand, mainly for the purpose of maintaining full employment, are so strong at this stage that to abolish trade barriers in this sector would encounter a number of difficulties. Moreover, all PAFTA countries ought to provide free access for developing countries' products of this type. How to foster structural adjustment in this sector for the five Pacific countries as a whole by taking into consideration the expansion of trade with developing countries in Asia and Latin America is an important but difficult problem.

(v) The elimination of tariffs in itself would not greatly change trade in foodstuffs (the expected increase being limited to 4·5 per cent), since a number of non-tariff restrictions exist either openly or covertly. Protectionism for agriculture is unreasonably strong, especially in Japan and the United States. Should these protectionist attitudes be rationalised, however, PAFTA trade in food offers much scope for expansion through mutual readjustment. Here, too, attention should be paid to the interests of developing countries.

Thus, the five Pacific countries should take measures to expand production and trade of heavy manufactures and chemicals as well as raw materials, on the one hand, and on the other, measures to readjust production and trade of light manufactures and food. Also, consideration has to be given to the

94

readjustments necessary for increasing trade with developing countries in Asia and Latin America. It might be best to concentrate on the expansion of production and trade in heavy manufactures, chemicals and raw materials and refrain from pushing the abolition of protectionism in light manufacturing and agriculture, as a first step towards wider Pacific integration. If the expansion of growing sectors is sufficiently large and rapid, readjustments in the lagging sectors will follow smoothly without so much trouble. For this reason, the sectoral free-trade approach has much to recommend it as a first step.

In order to expand harmonious production and horizontal trade in these growth sectors within the Pacific area, the elimination of tariffs should work effectively, but by itself it will not be enough. The free movement of capital and provision of larger markets or, in other words, the dynamic effects of economic integration should be promoted deliberately.

Effects of global tariff reductions

It is beyond our capacity for the time being, although admittedly very important, to estimate rigorously the effects of the Kennedy Round negotiations concluded in June 1967. Here a very rough estimation is attempted in order to show that even the largest global tariff reduction on the scale of the Kennedy Round would bring about a much smaller expansion of trade for the five Pacific countries than the establishment of PAFTA.

In making this estimate, it is assumed, first, that the elasticity of imports (and exports) with regard to the reduction of tariffs is the same as that adopted for each country's trade with PAFTA. Secondly, the rate of tariff reductions was 100 per cent in the case of PAFTA, while it is assumed here to be 25 per cent for food, 30 per cent for light manufactures, and 35 per cent both for raw materials and for heavy manufactures and chemicals, for the Kennedy Round negotiations. Thirdly, it is assumed that all the countries in Europe, i.e. the United Kingdom, the E.E.C. and other Western Europe, reduce tariffs.

Because of these assumptions, the estimates result in an overvaluation of the actual effects of the Kennedy Round tariff

95

reductions. Our estimates indicate the maximum likely effect of the global tariff reductions. Results are shown in Table 3.8.

Firstly, it should be noted that the rate of increase in trade due to tariff reductions is far larger in the case of the formation of PAFTA than in the case of the Kennedy Round. In the former

Table 3.8. Comparison of Static Effects of PAFTA and the Kennedy Round

		(a) PAFTA		(b) Kennedy Round	
		Value of increase (million/ $U.S.)	Rate of increase relative to total trade (per cent)	Value of increase (million/ $U.S.)	Rate of increase relative to total trade (per cent)
a. United States	Ex.	2,301·7	8·40	1,483·0	5·41
	Im.	2,283·2	10·65	1,711·8	7·99
	Bal.	18·5		−228·8	
b. Canada	Ex.	855·4	10·02	369·8	4·33
	Im.	1,480·8	18·49	651·1	8·13
	Bal.	−625·4		−281·4	
c. Japan	Ex.	1,743·1	20·62	741·0	8·77
	Im.	430·7	5·27	278·2	3·41
	Bal.	1,312·4		462·8	
d. Australia	Ex.	64·5	2·17	39·6	1·33
	Im.	650·6	19·29	504·7	14·96
	Bal.	−586·1		−465·1	
e. New Zealand	Ex.	22·1	2·19	15·4	1·53
	Im.	139·7	14·46	102·6	10·62
	Bal.	−117·6		−87·2	
Pacific countries	Ex.	4,986·8	10·31	2,648·8	5·48
	Im.	4,985·0	11·88	3,248·4	7·74
	Bal.	0		−599·6	
1965: Total exports		48,371·0			
Total imports		41,948·0			
Balance		6,423·0			

Source: Based on data and methods described in the text.

case, the total intra-areal trade of the five Pacific countries in 1965 would increase by 10·3 per cent and 11·9 per cent respectively for total exports to and imports from the world, while in the latter case the increase would be 5·5 per cent[9] and 7·7 per cent respectively. This suggests that complete regional trade liberalisation would be better than partial free trade in respect of the world market for the five Pacific countries as a whole, and for each of them separately.

Secondly, balance of payments effects too would be more advantageous in the case of PAFTA than in the case of global tariff reductions. In the former case, the balance of increments between exports and imports would be zero for the five Pacific countries taken together, while it would be in deficit by $U.S. 600 million in the latter case. For each country, it may be better to compare in both cases the ratio of imbalance to the sum of incremental exports and imports. The ratio would be 60·4 per cent in the case of PAFTA and 45·4 per cent in the case of global tariff reductions for Japan, 0·4 per cent and − 7·2 per cent for the United States, − 26·8 per cent and − 27·6 per cent for Canada, − 82·0 per cent and − 85·4 per cent for Australia, and − 72·7 per cent and − 73·9 per cent for New Zealand. These disadvantageous trade-balance effects in the case of global tariff reductions are due to the fact that a group of countries (i.e. developing countries and socialist countries) does not reduce tariffs but is allowed a 'free ride' on the Pacific countries' tariff reductions. The more favourable effects of establishing PAFTA as compared with global tariff reductions deserve careful note by the five Pacific countries, particularly since another global negotiation of tariff reductions as large as the Kennedy Round is unlikely to take place in the coming ten years.

IV. *Transfer of Markets to Asian Agricultural Products*

The establishment of a 'rich man's club' as large as PAFTA would have particularly adverse effects, economic as well as political, on Asian developing countries. The 'trade-diverting' effects of a PAFTA scheme might work against Asian interests. If this happened, the establishment of PAFTA would be extremely detrimental to Asian developing countries.

But let us suppose that the elimination of tariffs among PAFTA countries were extended to Asian products under a most-favoured-nation clause. Since imports from Asian developing countries are concentrated in primary products and light manufactures, the latter of which have been increasing but still remain small, the increase in imports for PAFTA countries would be very limited, unless the present export capacity of Asian developing countries is strengthened.

According to our estimation, imports from Asian developing countries would increase by $U.S. 425 million in the United States, $U.S. 27 million in Canada, $U.S. 50 million in Japan, $U.S. 58 million in Australia, $U.S. 11 million in New Zealand, and $U.S. 571 million in the five countries taken together, accounting for 16 per cent of their imports from Asian developing countries in 1965. This is not a large sum. For the five countries, the estimated increase in imports would be $U.S. 44 million in food, $U.S. 32 million in raw materials, $U.S. 371 million in light manufactures, and $U.S. 124 million in heavy manufactures and chemicals.

These estimates suggest that the liberalisation of trade and free market access for Asian developing countries' products would not help much to foster their trade growth. Besides the liberalisation of trade, stronger measures for widening markets through structural adjustment in the advanced Pacific countries themselves and for assistance in increasing the export capacity of Asian developing countries would be necessary. These stronger measures could not be pursued unless consolidated action was made possible through the establishment of PAFTA.

There are two main problems to be faced in the promotion of trade expansion from developing countries within the region. On the one hand, there is some competitiveness between exports of primary products and light manufactures from developed and developing countries within the region. On the other hand, superior competitive power and greater trade expansion by developed countries appear to inhibit trade expansion from developing countries.

Take, for example, Japan's imports of primary products. In pre-war days, soybean was imported from mainland China and rice was exclusively imported from Formosa and Korea. Nowadays, however, soybean and rice are imported from the United States. This does not represent all of the changes witnessed. Since the liberalisation of Japanese trade after 1960, primary goods are increasingly imported from the advanced Pacific countries, whose supplies are better in quality, cheaper in price, better in quality control, and more punctual in delivery. For instance, the share of sugar imports from Australia increased from 8·1 per cent in 1959 to 20·7 per cent in 1963, while the share of maize imports from the United States increased from 13·8 per cent in 1960 to 41·1 per cent in 1963. Sorghum was first imported in 1961 and imports increased rapidly. Now more than 99 per cent of Japan's requirements are purchased from the United States. As for raw cotton, however, there were wide fluctuations in the percentages imported from various countries; the import share for the United States was 22·9 per cent in 1959 and 31·6 per cent in 1963. In the case of mineral products, imports of iron ore from the United States, Canada and Australia increased from 13·4 per cent in 1959 to 15·2 per cent in 1963, with rapid increases in imports from Australia after that date. In the case of copper ore, imports from Canada and Australia increased sharply from 21·3 per cent in 1959 to 46·5 per cent in 1963. Coking coal was overwhelmingly imported from the United States, Canada and Australia.

The tendency for reduced imports of primary goods from developing countries is not limited only to Japan. According to the GATT investigation, imports of agricultural products into industrial areas combined from all sources expanded by nearly 40 per cent between 1953–5 and 1961–3. While imports originating from industrial countries themselves increased by about 60 per cent and those coming from Australia, New Zealand and South Africa, taken together, about as fast as average, imports of agricultural commodities originating in the other non-industrial countries expanded in volume by only one-fifth, i.e. three times less rapidly than agricultural trade among industrial countries.[10] More particularly, net exports from South-east Asia fell by nearly one-quarter between 1953–5 and 1960–2. GATT points out that the increase in consumption of agricultural products in developing countries themselves is one of the factors causing decreased exports from those countries. At the same time, however, it also noted that there was room left for the expansion of production capable of increasing both exports and consumption in the developing countries if only the appropriate policies were taken. If the share of developing countries in the markets of industrial countries had remained the same as in 1953–5, their export earnings would have been

99

about $U.S. 2,000 million higher in 1961–3. Furthermore, their imports of agricultural products, excluding non-commercial deliveries, amounted to nearly $U.S. 4,000 million in 1963: an expansion in the production and trade of these countries would tend to permit a reduction in deliveries from industrial countries.

Perhaps it would be very difficult politically to change the sources of supply for mineral products, which are influenced by the availability of deposits, difficulties in extraction and transportation, etc. However, so far as agricultural products such as food and raw materials are concerned, there is probably room for transferring the sources of supply from advanced countries to developing countries. This is the field in which consolidated policy by advanced Pacific countries is very necessary.

The size of the market which could be transferred from produce in advanced Pacific countries to those in Asian developing countries can be estimated roughly. The estimate is based on the data for the 1960s and confined to agricultural products.

We assume two steps in the transfer. In the first round, the advanced Pacific countries refrain from importing agricultural products as much as possible from other advanced countries and transfer sources of supply to Asian developing countries. At the same time, the advanced countries abstain from expanding agricultural production for their own consumption and increase demand for Asian produce. It could take ten years or more to complete the first round. The transfer of supply sources is examined for those agricultural products which can be produced in Asian developing countries competitively in terms of quality, price, delivery, etc., with the goods of advanced countries. Between five and ten years should be allowed for developing countries to improve productivity and to increase export capacity. For advanced countries too, some length of time is required for adjusting industrial structure and employment.

In the second round, a further transfer of markets to developing countries should take place if the advanced Pacific countries refrained from exporting agricultural products to countries outside the area, especially to Western Europe, and curtailed their production to the limit of 'minimum self-sufficiency' which may be determined from optimum allocation of resources, considerations of national defence, etc. Our investigation is confined to the first round, although the effects of the second round would be far greater and require wider structural adjustment in advanced countries not only in the Pacific area but also in Western Europe.

Data for our study are available in FAO, *Commodity Review, 1964, Special Supplement: Trade in Agricultural Commodities in the United Nations Development Decade.* The coverage of trade statistics is sufficient (three-quarters) in the case of food (including beverages and tobacco) and agricultural raw materials originating from developing countries. One defect of FAO statistics is the fact that trade of Australia, New Zealand and South Africa is combined together and, consequently, South African trade has to be included in the total of advanced Pacific countries. Since the importance of South African trade is very limited, it does not result in serious bias in our estimation.

We have selected eight agricultural products (cereals, maize, rice, sugar, tobacco, oil and fat, raw cotton, and raw hide) as items in the range produced competitively both in advanced Pacific countries and Asian developing countries, and markets for which could be transferred from the former's to the latter's produce. Special products of developing countries such as coffee, cocoa, tea, bananas, rubber, jute and other hard fibres are excluded, since they are not competitive products. For the same reason dairy products, wool and wheat are also excluded.

The expected increase in demand for South-east Asian exports of agricultural products was estimated independently. Our forecast is based on forecasts similar to those undertaken by ECAFE, FAO and the Institute of Asian Economic Affairs.

Our estimates suggest that increased agricultural exports to Japan in consequence of these measures would amount to $U.S. 672 million, $U.S. 317 million of which would comprise the transfer effect and $U.S. 355 million the effect of demand growth up to 1970. Increased agricultural exports to other Pacific countries would amount to $U.S. 408 million, of which $U.S. 183 million would comprise the transfer effect and $U.S. 225 million the effect of growth in demand (see Table 3.9). In other words, since exports of agricultural products from South-east Asia to the advanced Pacific countries amounted to $U.S. 1,160 million per year in the period 1959–61, Asian exports would almost double on the completion of the first round of transfers. As mentioned before, FAO statistics cover only 75 per cent of foodstuffs and 86 per cent of agricultural raw materials, and so the presumed figure can be inflated accordingly. That is, exports of agricultural products from Southeast Asia to the advanced Pacific countries can be expected to increase from $U.S. 1,414 million in 1959–61 average to $U.S. 2,750 million in 1970.

Table 3.9. Estimates of the Transfer of Agricultural Markets in Favour of Asian Developing Countries (million U.S. dollars)

	Transferable amount in 1959–61 (average)	Demand increase in the five advanced Pacific countries during the subsequent ten years	Total
(a) Food (incl. beverages and tobacco)	177	285	462
(b) Raw materials	323	295	618
(c) Total	500	580	1,080

The possibility for import substitution in Asian developing countries should also be examined. In 1959–61, imports from the advanced Pacific countries amounted to $U.S. 1,040 million, of which foodstuffs accounted for $U.S. 740 million and raw materials for $U.S. 300 million. If Asian developing countries succeeded in substituting a large proportion of these imports for domestic production in the process of the first round, the effect would be equivalent to that deriving from the market transfer.

The estimated increase in Asian developing countries' trade is not insignificant. The consequent trade growth would surely help to improve the balance of payments position of Asian countries. According to the ECAFE projection,[11] based upon an assumed growth rate of national income at 5 per cent, some $U.S. 5,000 million of deficit in the balance of trade is projected for the year 1970. This deficit could be reduced to $U.S. 2,500 million if these proposals were realised. The remaining trade gap would be filled if similar measures were taken for mining products as well as labour-intensive light manufactures.

It should be remembered that the trade gap of some $U.S. 5,000 million forecast by ECAFE is a burden for advanced countries, mainly in the Pacific region, and that it would have to be filled through economic assistance and other measures. As compared with this, the impact of our scheme upon the advanced Pacific countries would be far less burdensome. For Japan, the only requirement is to transfer sources of supply of agricultural imports from advanced Pacific countries to Asian developing countries. However, Japan would bear the cost of expensive imports for some time until Asian productivity improved. Other Pacific countries would lose exports of food to the extent of $U.S. 95 million or 1·7 per cent of their total exports of food, and exports of agricultural raw materials to the extent of $U.S. 90 million or 1·8 per cent of their total exports of these products.

Financial and technical assistance to Asian developing countries would also be necessary to improving productivity and expanding the productive capacity of Asian agriculture in addition to the required structural adjustments in advanced Pacific countries. Such assistance would be a small burden and could be used efficiently and beneficially both for advanced and developing countries in the region. This argument will be developed in subsequent chapters, where the problems associated with promoting Asian exports of labour-intensive manufactures will also be discussed in detail.

Whether or not a Pacific Free Trade Area among the United States, Canada, Japan, Australia and New Zealand is established, the transfer of markets in favour of Asian developing countries could be pursued independently, since it presents a quite promising means for improving their balance of trade as well as their national income. Moreover, it would be an economical and effective means of supporting economic development in Asian countries and promoting trade between advanced Pacific countries and Asian developing countries. As will be argued in subsequent chapters, it is essential, however, that consolidated action by advanced Pacific countries be taken if these measures are to be given proper and balanced effect.

For this reason, the establishment of PAFTA is a desirable precondition to effective aid and trade assistance policies. Only under this circumstance will the burdens and benefits be fairly shared, and the development effects substantial.

4 Trade Preferences for Developing Countries

I. *Introduction*

Among the most important themes of the Second United Nations Conference on Trade and Development in New Delhi in 1968 was the discussion of schemes for general trade preferences for developing countries. Japan is one of the developed countries in the process of defining her attitude on this question. Over the last few years, there has been lively debate among Japanese Government officials, businessmen and academic economists about what attitude Japan might best adopt. In November 1967, the Japanese Government finally lined up beside other O.E.C.D. countries and opted for the scheme of general trade preferences. The estimates of the impact of preferences on Japanese trade, spelled out in this chapter, played a not insignificant part in leading Japanese opinion towards this more positive position.[1]

General trade preferences will have trade-creating effects, trade-diverting effects and dynamic effects. This chapter aims, firstly, to assess the impact of preferences for developing countries upon Japan's imports and exports and thereby to provide some of the basic information necessary to more effective trade-policy decision-making. Secondly, alternative preference schemes, such as the advance-cut and tariff quota proposals, are compared. Finally, I put forward a new suggestion, a proposal for aid-cum-preferences, which may commend itself to developed and developing countries alike.

II. *The Trade-creation Effect: Increases in Japan's Imports*

Japan's imports of manufactures and semi-manufactures from developing countries are differentiated from imports originating in developed countries in kind and quality. The increase in Japanese imports due to the extension of trade preferences for developing countries can therefore be estimated using a familiar model. The trade-diversion effects on developed-country exporters are neglected and attention focused on the trade-creation effects on Japanese imports.

In Fig. 4.1, D represents Japan's (or any preference-giving country's) import demand schedule for some developing-country export commodity, X; S represents the developing countries' export supply schedule; and S' represents the tariff-ridden export schedule.

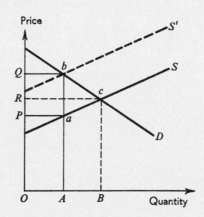

Figure 4.1: Trade-creation effects.

Before the extension of preferences, Japan imported OA units of X at price OP, the value of imports from developing countries being $OPaA$. In Japanese markets, commodity X is sold at the price OQ, higher than the developing countries' export price by the extent of the tariff, t, Japanese tariff revenue being $PQba$.

Now, suppose tariffs on imports from developing countries are abolished. The tariff preference margin, β, then equals unity.[2] The price of the developing-country export rises from P to R. The rate of price increase is shown by:

$$\pi_x = \frac{\eta_j}{\eta_j + \epsilon_u}\left(\beta \cdot \frac{t}{1+t}\right). \tag{1}$$

The price of X in Japan, inclusive of tariff, falls from Q, or $(1+t)P$, to R. The rate of price decrease is shown by:

$$\pi_m = \frac{\epsilon_u}{\eta_j + \epsilon_u}\left(\beta \cdot \frac{t}{1+t}\right) \tag{2}$$

where η_j is the price elasticity of Japan's import demand and ϵ_u is the price elasticity of developing countries' export supply.

Table 4.1. Effects of General Preference on Japan's Imports
from Developing Countries:
An Estimate Based upon Trade Figures in 1964

Commodity group	M ($'000)	t (%)	M_u ($'000)	ΔM_u ($'000)	$\dfrac{\Delta M_u}{M_u}$ (%)	π_x (%)	η_j	ϵ_u
Plywood	211	20·0	4	–	–	8·33	0·7	0·7
Cotton yarn and thread	45	6·4	24	1	4·2	3·02	0·7	0·7
Yarn and thread of synthetic fibres	1,386	20·0	450	64	14·3	8·33	0·7	0·7
Cotton fabrics, woven	2,635	10·0	910	91	10·2	4·54	1·2	1·2
Floor coverings	1,997	30·0	81	29	35·8	11·29	2·1	2·2
Clothing	7,752	26·4	1,076	352	32·8	10·22	2·1	2·2
Footwear	1,227	26·4	87	28	32·2	10·22	2·1	2·2
Articles of plastic materials	4,193	25·0	95	30	31·6	9·78	2·1	2·2
Travel goods, handbags	556	20·0	42	11	26·2	8·15	2·1	2·2
Small-wares and toilet articles	2,917	35·7	341	140	41·0	12·87	2·1	2·2
Children's toys	12,210	20·0	328	86	26·2	8·15	2·1	2·2
Lighters	1,343	25·4	255	81	31·7	9·91	2·1	2·2
Total or average	36,472		3,693	913	24·7	8·56		

Source: Based on data and methods described in the text.

If the original value of Japan's imports is denoted by M,[3] the increase in imports is shown by:

$$\Delta M = \pi_x(1 + \epsilon_u)M. \tag{3}$$

Using this model, estimates of the increase in Japanese imports in consequence of the extension of 100 per cent tariff preferences were made for twelve sensitive commodities of importance to developing countries. The initial estimates were

107

made on a disaggregated basis, but they are aggregated and summarised in Table 4.1. One important problem was the estimation of the price elasticities, η_j and ϵ_u. As shown in Table 4.1, the twelve commodities analysed were classified into three broad groups – lightly processed intermediate manufactures, highly processed intermediate manufactures, and finished manufactures – and three broad elasticity bands assigned accordingly. The precise values of these elasticity bands are ultimately guesswork, but their orders of magnitude are probably accurate enough.[4]

In 1964, developing-country exports of these twelve commodities to Japan were valued at $U.S. 3·69 million, which represented a 10 per cent share in the relevant Japanese markets. The estimates set out in Table 4.1 suggest that if tariffs were abolished on developing-country exports to Japan (that is, β equalled unity), they would expand by $U.S. 0·91 million, or 24·7 per cent, on 1964 trade figures.[5] Although the percentage increase appears large, the size of the increase is relatively insignificant when compared with annual increases in Japanese exports of the order of $U.S. 1,500 million. The fact is that Japan still maintains a strong comparative advantage in traditional labour-intensive manufacturing industries of the type most competitive with potential export industries in developing countries.

In Japan, none the less, there remains a strong fear that certain traditional labour-intensive industries, typically comprising small-scale firms concentrated in particular industrial districts, would be severely damaged by the extension of tariff preferences. This fear tends to be exaggerated both by the vested interests concerned and by the Ministry of International Trade and Industry. It is true that in recent years, Japan's imports of manufactured goods from Hong Kong, Taiwan, Korea, Singapore and India have been increasing rapidly, but they are still insignificant. However, taking this trend into account, and broadening the commodity coverage, it might be that around $U.S. 50 million worth of Japanese imports could be affected by the extension of trade preferences. If tariffs against developing-country exports were completely eliminated, imports would increase by $U.S. 13 million only. A 50 per cent tariff cut is probably a more realistic possibility, and besides some commodities are likely to be excepted. On this basis, the increase in Japanese imports would be somewhat less than $U.S. 6·5 million. There seem no strong grounds for Japan to oppose the provision of general trade preferences for fear of unmanageable increases in her imports.

III. *The Trade-diversion Effects: Decreases in Japan's Exports*

A more serious problem for Japan is that her exports, particularly to North American markets, might suffer from the trade-diversion effects of trade preferences extended by other developed countries to developing countries. A more complicated model is required in order to estimate the effects of both trade creation and trade diversion in a given developed-country market, such as the United States.

Suppose Japan competes with developing countries in the export of some manufactured commodity X to the American market. In Fig. 4.2, D represents the American demand schedule; S_j Japan's export supply schedule; and S_u the developing countries' export supply schedule.

By summation, a composite export supply schedule, $S_u + S_j$, is obtained. If tariffs are imposed against all imports by the United States, the tariff-ridden export supply schedules are represented by S_j', S_u', and $S_u' + S_j'$. If tariffs are imposed only against Japanese imports, $S_u + S_j'$ is the composite export supply schedule. And $D - S_j'$ represents United States demand for X from developing countries alone.

Before the introduction of trade preferences, equilibrium is determined at b where D and $S_u' + S_j'$ intersect. This equilibrium is exactly equivalent to that described in Fig. 4.1. The United States imports OA units of which Oj are supplied by Japan and the remainder, jA equal to Ue, are supplied by developing countries. The international price of imports is OP, whilst the price inclusive of tariff is OQ.

Suppose that tariffs on commodities imported from developing countries are abolished (that is, the preference margin, β, is unity) and tariffs on Japanese imports remain unchanged.

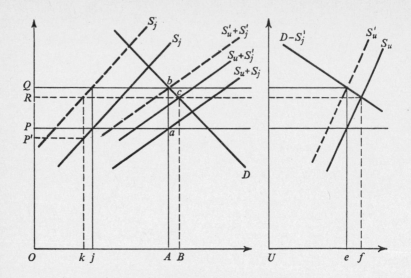

Figure 4.2: Trade-creation and trade diversion effects.

After the extension of trade preferences, a new equilibrium is reached at c where D and $S_u + S_j'$ intersect. America increases her imports from OA to OB, of which Ok are supplied by Japan and the remainder, kB equal to Uf, are supplied by developing countries. The price of imports, inclusive of the tariff on Japanese supplies, falls from OQ to OR. Japanese export prices are forced down from OP to OP', equivalent to the decrease in the American import price inclusive of tariff, that is, QR equals PP'.

Thus, the quantity of American imports increases by ΔM^* owing to the trade-creation effect of preferential tariff reductions, while the quantity of Japanese exports decreases by ΔM_j^* owing to the trade-diversion effects. Developing-country exports increase by ΔM_u^*, which is the sum of the trade-creation and trade-diversion effects.

$$\Delta M_u^* = \Delta M^* + \Delta M_j^*. \tag{4}$$

The export price from developing countries after the extension of preferences, OR in Fig. 4.2, is shown by $\{1 + (1 - \beta)t\}$ $P(1 + \pi_x)$, or simply $P(1 + \pi_x)$, if β equals unity. This will equal the price of exports from Japan inclusive of the tariff, $P(1+t)(1-\pi_m)$.

$$P(1+t)(1-\pi_m) = \{1+(1-\beta)t\} P(1+\pi_x). \qquad (5)$$

The rate of decrease in the United States import price inclusive of the tariff will be:

$$\pi_m = \frac{\alpha\epsilon_u}{\eta+\alpha\epsilon_u+(1-\alpha)\epsilon_j} \cdot \frac{t \cdot \beta}{1+t} \qquad (6)$$

and the rate of increase in the export price from developing countries will be:

$$\pi_x = \frac{\eta+(1-\alpha)\epsilon_j}{\eta+\alpha\epsilon_u+(1-\alpha)\epsilon_j} \cdot \frac{t \cdot \beta}{1+t} \qquad (7)$$

where η is the price elasticity of American import demand, ϵ_u and ϵ_j are the price elasticities of export supply from developing countries and Japan respectively, and α is the developing countries' share in American markets.

Finally, the decrease in the value of Japan's exports, ΔM_j, and the increase in the value of developing exports, ΔM_u, will be:

$$\Delta M_j = \pi_m(1+\epsilon_j)M_j \qquad (8)$$

$$\Delta M_u = \pi_x(1+\epsilon_u)M_u. \qquad (9)$$

Table 4.2 records nineteen manufactured commodities of importance to developing countries which compete with Japanese exports in the American market. In 1964, United States imports of these commodities were valued at $U.S. 1,600 million. Japan supplied $U.S. 540 million and developing countries supplied $U.S. 465 million. The nineteen items cover almost all the manufactured and semi-manufactured goods for which developing countries, as well as Japan, seek larger markets in the United States. The elasticity assumptions,[6] relevant American tariff rates, and results of calculations using the model described above are also detailed in Table 4.2.

If the preference margin, β, is unity, it appears that developing countries would increase their exports to America by $U.S. 176 million, or 37·8 per cent on 1964 trade figures. The rise in developing-country export prices, π_x, would average

Table 4.2. Effects of General Preferences on Exports from Japan and Developing Countries in American Markets: An Estimate Based upon Trade Figures in 1964

Commodity group	M ($'000)	t (%)	M_j ($'000)	$-\Delta M_j$ ($'000)	$\dfrac{-\Delta M_j}{M_j}$ (%)	$-\pi_m$ (%)	M_u ($'000)	ΔM_u ($'000)	$\dfrac{\Delta M_u}{M_u}$ (%)	π_x (%)	η	ϵ_j	ϵ_u
Cotton fabrics, woven	104,998	12·9	31,251	1,656	5·3	2·31	44,200	10,431	23·6	10·28	1·4	1·2	1·2
Yarn of wool	21,303	25·0	4,621	9	0·2	0·14	322	136	42·2	24·83	0·9	0·7	0·7
Woollen fabrics, woven	80,372	48·9	46,532	419	0·9	0·39	2,011	223	11·1	48·31	1·4	1·2	1·2
Jute fabrics, woven	179,655	12·4	753	83	11·0	4·79	154,582	24,888	16·1	7·01	1·4	1·2	1·2
Floor coverings	54,373	22·5	27,151	1,901	7·0	2·20	13,987	8,868	63·4	19·80	2·5	2·2	2·2
Clothing	451,836	22·8	113,414	9,980	8·8	2·76	144,463	89,711	62·1	19·40	2·5	2·2	2·2
Manufactures of leather	7,126	10·0	1,339	31	2·3	0·73	1,235	363	29·4	9·19	2·5	2·2	2·2
Footwear	141,436	19·6	50,319	554	1·1	0·34	6,816	4,178	61·3	19·17	2·5	2·2	2·2
Sporting goods	38,578	20·2	13,807	166	1·2	0·37	1,847	1,167	63·2	19·76	2·5	2·2	2·2
Children's toys	88,196	31·4	54,893	3,458	6·3	1·98	15,682	14,443	92·1	28·79	2·5	2·2	2·2
Articles of rubber	40,249	10·7	3,837	1	0·02	0·01	88	22	24·6	10·69	1·4	1·2	1·2
Plywood	123,238	20·0	50,890	2,799	5·5	3·24	54,922	15,049	27·4	16·10	0·9	0·7	0·7
Cement	9,235	5·0	229	2	0·7	0·41	1,855	145	7·8	4·56	0·9	0·7	0·7
Glass	60,046	15·7	9,768	49	0·5	0·27	2,742	718	26·2	15·39	0·9	0·7	0·7
Glassware	34,159	27·6	2,916	41	1·4	0·45	1,575	1,362	86·5	27·02	2·5	2·2	2·2
Soaps	1,562	14·0	20	1	0·5	0·16	45	20	44·2	13·82	2·5	2·2	2·2
Sewing machines	61,041	10·0	36,616	22	0·06	0·02	367	117	31·9	9·98	2·5	2·2	2·2
Bicycles	29,668	30·0	6,058	12	0·2	0·07	218	209	95·7	29·91	2·5	2·2	2·2
Radio broadcast receivers	111,915	12·5	84,667	1,355	1·6	0·49	10,648	4,068	38·2	11·95	2·5	2·2	2·2
Total or average	1,578,923		539,070	22,538	4·1	1·96	465,531	176,118	37·8	18·26			

Source: Based on data and methods described in the text.

18·3 per cent. On the other hand, $U.S. 22·5 million or 4·1 per cent of Japanese exports would be diverted to developing countries and Japanese export prices would be forced down on average by 2·0 per cent. Thus, the United States would increase her imports by $U.S. 153·5 million or about 10 per cent on 1964 figures – the difference between the increase in developing countries' exports and the reduction in Japan's exports. The increase in American imports is the trade-creation effect of preferences resulting from the average fall of 2·0 per cent in American import prices inclusive of the tariff.

The question is, would the effect of trade diversion on Japanese exports be really serious? The Japanese Ministry of International Trade and Industry presented a very exaggerated estimate in early September 1967[7] which called forth considerable critical comment. It suggested that Japanese exports to developed-country markets valued at $U.S. 900 million would be affected by general trade preferences and that the loss of exports could be as large as $U.S. 135–180 million, since Japanese export prices would be forced down to the full extent of tariff reductions in order to maintain export volumes. This Ministry of International Trade and Industry estimate is fundamentally in error, since it completely neglects the probable increases in developed-country imports in consequence of tariff reductions. Where the import price inclusive of tariff is reduced by 15 or 20 per cent, the value of exports, both from developing countries and Japan, will increase to the extent that the price elasticity of developed-country import demand is greater than unity.

Interestingly, in mid-October 1967, the Japanese Ministry of Finance published another estimate of the effects of tariff preferences[8] which employed methods, and yielded results, similar to those found here. The Ministry of Finance estimate covers trade in six commodities additional to those analysed in Table 4.2 (cotton yarn and thread, manufactures of asbestos, furniture, leather, essential oil and resinoids, and electric fans) and is based on 1966 trade data. Japan's exports to the United States of the twenty-five commodities studied were $U.S. 702 million in 1966, and the Ministry of Finance estimated that they would fall by $U.S. 27·7 million or 4·0 per cent, with a 2·0 per cent fall in average export prices (π_m), if United States tariffs were completely eliminated on imports from developing countries. If these estimates are extended to include Japanese exports not only to the United States but also to Canada, the E.E.C., EFTA, Finland, Australia and New Zealand, the decrease in exports would amount to around $U.S. 40 million. This seems a fairly reasonable estimate.

Again, the trade-diversion effect of general trade preferences upon Japan would not be nearly so serious as is widely feared. If the preference margin, β, were 0·5 instead of unity, exports would fall by only $U.S. 20 million. This would, however, be greater than the increase in Japan's own imports of approximately $U.S. 6·5 million. Japan is, indeed, the only advanced country, with perhaps the exception of Italy, which exports traditional labour-intensive manufactures in competition with developing countries and is open to significant trade-diversion losses. It is for these reasons that, within the O.E.C.D., the Japanese Government has pressed for sharing the burden of tariff preferences, not only in terms of their effect through increasing imports but also in terms of their effect in diverting developed-country exports away to developing countries. How exactly this might be effected is a separate and difficult problem for the governments concerned.

Is there any means whereby Japan could overcome the trade-diversion effect of trade preferences and expand her exports along with, though more slowly than, developing countries? This, I feel, depends on the kind of trade preference scheme adopted.

IV. *Advance-cut* versus *Tariff Quota Preference Schemes*

Two alternative preference schemes have been presented to O.E.C.D. countries: the advance-cut plan advocated by the United States, and the tariff quota plan supported by E.E.C. countries. It has been suggested that the advance-cut preference scheme could be applied *either* by reducing tariffs on developing-country products to the full extent of concessions agreed under Kennedy Round negotiations *or* by reducing tariffs on developing-country products under negotiations between developing countries and developed countries within GATT, to be followed by a new round of negotiations among developed countries designed to effect the staged reduction of most-favoured-nation tariffs over five or ten years. Either way, the advance-cut plan ensures that general preferences are temporary and that they are consistent with progress towards global free trade. These are the significant merits of the advance-cut proposals.

On the other hand, the tariff quota scheme appears more open to protectionist abuses, and unlikely to promote trade liberalisation in developed countries. Quotas on selected commodities from particular developing-country sources would be subject to arbitrary alteration, and most-favoured-nation tariffs could even be raised to provide larger preference margins. Fundamentally, the tariff quota plan does not aim at progress towards global free trade but sets out to prevent 'market disruption' by developing-country products. From the standpoint of encouraging the expansion of world trade, the advance-cut proposals seem preferable.

From Japan's viewpoint also the advance-cut proposals seem superior to the tariff quota proposals. Under the tariff quota plan, Japan would suffer trade-diversion effects of the kind analysed above. On the other hand, if, as envisaged under the advance-cut plan, most-favoured-nation tariffs were gradually reduced, Japanese exports would expand along with exports from developing countries. In the early phases of implementing an advance-cut scheme, preference margins would induce trade diversion at Japan's expense. In later phases, as preference margins narrow and larger most-favoured-nation tariff reductions apply, the expansionary effect on Japanese exports would more than compensate for the losses from trade diversion, whilst developing-country exports would continue to expand because of the effects of scale economies and increased productivity or international competitiveness.

Permanent preferences, i.e. general preferences with no limitation in duration, are certainly more favourable to less developed countries than the advance-cut plan, but they will not be favoured by developed countries. It may be interesting, however, to illustrate the difference in effects of both schemes for the case of Japan.

Let us suppose that (1) America imported in the initial year $U.S. 600 million from Japan and $U.S. 400 million from developing countries, as she did, roughly, in 1964; (2) the American tariff level was 30 per cent *ad valorem*; (3) preferential margin equals 0·5 both under the advance-cut plan and the permanent preferences plan; (4) tariffs are reduced by 10 per cent every year for five years under the advance-cut plan but are reduced by 50 per cent from the first year under the permanent preferences plan; (5) the price elasticity of American import demand is taken as 2·5 and the price elasticity of export supply from Japan as 2·2 throughout the five years; and (6) the price elasticity of export supply from developing countries will increase from 1·1 in the first year to 1·65, 2·2, 2·75 and 3·3 in successive years.

Under these assumptions, over the whole five-year period, Japanese exports would fall by $U.S. 205 million or 6·8 per cent under the permanent preferences plan, whilst they would increase by $U.S. 306 million or 10·2 per cent under the advance-cut plan.

Exports of developing countries would increase by $U.S. 671 million or 33·4 per cent in the case of the permanent preferences plan and by $U.S. 514 million or 23·7 per cent in the case of the advance-cut plan.

American imports would increase by $U.S. 466 million, i.e. net of increase from developing countries and decrease from Japan, in the case of the permanent preferences plan, whilst they would increase by $U.S. 820 million, i.e. the sum of increase both from developing countries and Japan, in the case of the advance-cut plan.

Thus, Japan would not be harmed so much by the advance-cut as by the tariff quota plan and could even benefit from it provided developed countries ultimately undertook most-favoured-nation tariff reductions. Under the advance-cut plan, trade expansion among developed countries would offset the impact of trade diversion towards developing countries. Indeed, the Japanese Government should press for sharing the burden of trade diversion by insisting on most-favoured-nation tariff reductions among developed countries, particularly on those commodities on which she would suffer most trade diversion.

Japan has many interests in common with developing

countries. She still depends heavily on the export of traditional labour-intensive manufactures in competition with developing countries, but, like them, she desires freer access to developed-country markets for these exports. If the second variant of the advance-cut proposals were applied again and again, it would serve to break down protectionism in high-wage developed countries. It is important to emphasise that for developing countries too, the benefits of trade preference schemes derive not so much from *discrimination* in tariff treatment but more from the *reduction* of tariffs in developed countries.

V. *A Scheme for Aid-cum-Trade Preferences*

Trade preferences for developing countries are justifiable if divergence from the principle of non-discrimination within GATT is temporary and they foster liberalisation of world trade. They are positively desirable if they encourage transformation in the international division of labour in such a way as to strengthen specialisation in the export of labour-intensive exports from developing countries.[9] But what this study and others have shown is that the static effects of preference schemes are not likely to be substantial.[10] The prospects are generally discouraging for developing countries. The benefits for them may be even too small to justify the cost of carrying out the cumbersome administration of preferential treatment. The increased earning power of developing countries which results from trade preference is certainly not likely to fill their huge foreign exchange gap.[11]

It may be true that if the effective rates of protection, which are on average 1·5 or 2 times the nominal tariff rates,[12] and the dynamic effects of preferences, are taken into account, the favourable effects of general preferences for less developed countries would be more substantial. But these effects depend heavily upon developed-country assistance in the form of capital, know-how and management for establishing and rationalising productive facilities in developing countries.

Moreover, there are conflicting interests among the potential preference-receivers. The main interest of the less developed

117

among the developing countries is not so much preferential tariff treatment on manufactured exports as, first, the expansion of traditional primary commodity exports, and second, the initiation of industrialisation with heavy dependence on aid from developed countries.

In fact, developed countries have been reluctantly led towards the provision of general trade preferences, not because they expect any substantial benefits to flow to developing countries but because they recognise the political expedience of providing them.

An aid-cum-preference scheme could offer more benefits to developing countries. Aid, linked directly to preferential tariff treatment, appears consistent with the Prebisch report's emphasis on the infant-industry argument for preferences.[13] Firstly, directly productive aid in the form of capital goods, advanced techniques of production, managerial know-how and worker training should be provided to developing countries on an increasingly large scale if the efficiency of new export-oriented industries, primary as well as manufacturing, is to be improved to the point where they become increasingly competitive in world markets. Secondly, developed countries should provide preferential treatment, say for five or ten years, to developing-country exports launched with the help of directly productive aid. Preferences aimed at ensuring wider markets would serve as a sort of aid 'after-care', and might well be regarded as indispensable to realising the full benefits of aid. It is important that the provision of preferences should be closely linked with the provision of aid, since either is likely to be ineffective and result in a waste of resources if applied independently.

The aid-cum-preference scheme need not be confined to manufactured goods. It could also be useful for agricultural and mineral commodities of interest to developing countries. Commonly, however, developed-country tariffs on these latter products are very low or non-existent and there is little margin for granting preferences. In such cases, developed-country governments could provide a subsidy on imports from developing countries for some specific period, say five years, until competitiveness is sufficiently well established.

In the past, Japan has stressed 'development investment for

118

import' as a useful form of aid to assist primary product exports from developing countries. The development of maize exports from Thailand to Japan is one successful example. It is in Japan's interests to switch purchases of raw materials and food-stuffs from developed to developing countries as much as possible, particularly since Japan usually has export surpluses with developing countries. The main difficulty, of course, is that developing countries are presently more expensive and less reliable sources of supply than developed countries. Large-scale aid-cum-trade preferences could help overcome this difficulty.

The aid-cum-preference scheme might well be subject to criticism from developing countries on the grounds that it is not a 'general' preference scheme but, of its nature, would have to be selective of both commodities and countries. However, if preferences are justifiable on infant-industry grounds, it seems appropriate for them to be both selective and temporary. In any case, the so-called general trade preference schemes discussed above would involve selectivity in practice, and the beneficial effects of their 'generality' are likely to be nullified by selective administration.

The aid-cum-preference scheme involves the provision of aid by developed countries, through the use of government funds and private capital, to selected industries in developing countries, and the import and marketing of the output by developed countries. The developed country should not only be ready to provide trade preferences but also press other developed countries to provide equivalent preferences[14] (a procedure similar in principle to the multilateralisation of bilateral negotiations through most-favoured-nation treatment within GATT). In this way, the generality of the preferences could be assured for preference-giving countries. Although industries to which aid and preferences are extended may be limited, the industries selected would be fully insured by developed countries in the production and marketing of their output. Thus, the aid-cum-preference scheme is potentially more useful than 'general' preference schemes which are only formally general in character. It should be remembered, for example, why British preferences have benefited developing countries. The benefits derived not so much from the preferences themselves but from all-round assistance with the provision of capital, management and marketing skills. [15]

Certainly, there are many technicalities of the aid-cum-preference proposal that require further detailed study. For example, what should be the range of aid with which trade preferences are linked? How could preferences be linked with aid through multinational organisations? These are questions which need to be studied along with ways in which to soften the terms upon which aid is provided, by developed and developing countries alike.

5 PAFTA and Asian Developing Countries

I. *A New Stage in the North–South Problem*

In actuality, of course, the Second United Nations Conference on Trade and Development at New Delhi in February–March 1968 ended with frustration and disappointment for the developing countries.[1] This was not surprising, since it was held at a very unfavourable time when the developed countries were involved in difficulties of their own such as the devaluation of sterling, the gold crisis, and a rising tide of restrictive and protectionist foreign trade and aid policies in the United States. The main positive achievement of the conference was an agreement to proceed with the establishment of a 'general system of preferences' for developing-country exports of manufactures, to be worked out in the course of 1968–9 and, hopefully, implemented in 1970.

An important question arises. How effective is a global approach to the North–South problem likely to be? It is doubtful whether a multi-country meeting of this scale can substitute for more intensive negotiations between a small number of countries. The problems raised by the persistence of the basic cleavages of interest both within and between the two groups of developed and less developed countries are multiplied by more than the number of countries involved.[2] Even if agreement could be reached, concessions are likely to be severely limited and of nominal value. It is urgently necessary to formulate a more effective and constructive approach to the problem. A regional approach in which like-minded countries, from both the developed and less developed group, foster trade development among themselves seems more promising. However, a regional approach cannot be a substitute for a global approach to development problems. Rather, it represents an effective step towards the global approach.

Currently, the North–South problem seems to be facing a turning point: there is a shift in emphasis from aid and trade expansion of a 'vent-for-surplus' type to that of a 'structural adjustment' type.

In the last decade, less developed countries sought as much aid as possible from the developed countries. This aid was mainly used to provide social overhead capital and to fill the gap in the trade balance incurred by accelerated imports of capital equipment. In short, it was not really directed towards increasing exports. However, substantial foreign debts have accumulated in many developing countries and repayments and service charges surpass new borrowings. Thus, in addition to increased aid and a softening of terms of aid, the expansion of exports from developing countries is an urgent task.

Since economic development in many developing countries has been confined to investment of the 'infrastructural' type and the establishment of import-substituting industries, exports have continued to consist mainly of traditional primary products. These exports have suffered from a declining importance in total world trade and also from severe fluctuation in their prices. Prospects for these exports look even worse because of the rapid growth in the supply of synthetic substitutes and the world-wide tendency towards trade liberalisation, both of which make things even harder for the low-quality, high-cost type of exports of the developing countries.

Thus, developing countries must turn to the expansion of export-oriented productive activities. The expansion of exports, not only in speciality tropical goods but also in certain labour-intensive manufactured and semi-manufactured goods, appropriate to the factor endowment ratio in developing countries, now seems the most promising line of economic development. Developing countries have to shift the emphasis from receiving aid to the expansion of exports, and from agricultural exports to a structural transformation of their economies towards the export of manufactures.

Developed countries should take appropriate measures to facilitate structural transformation in developing countries. However, in the last decade, developed countries have confined themselves significantly to providing the 'vent-for-surplus'-type aid. United States aid in the form of surplus agricultural products under Public Law 480 is one good example. To take another example, Japanese aid has so far been provided mainly for the purpose of increasing her own exports of heavy manufactures and chemicals. Japanese reparations to Asian countries up to about 1960 were directed towards stimulating the expansion of newly established heavy industries and at the same time absorbing a large amount of unemployed labour. Aid from developed countries has been provided partly because there has been surplus produce or surplus capacity in resources, and aid has served as the vent for these surpluses.

Since about 1960, developed countries, including Japan, have been subject to more inflationary pressure. Aid of the vent-for-surplus type could not be continued easily. A new concept of aid and new aid policies have become necessary.

New types of aid and access for the exports of the developing countries to the markets of the developed countries should be provided by means of the structural adjustment of industries in developed countries. The developed countries would be better off substituting the production of a number of domestic industries for imports from the developing countries. There are certainly some 'declining' industries in the developed countries which are so old and inefficient that, from all the criteria of comparative advantage and efficiency in resource allocation, it would be better to phase them out of existence. Productive resources thus released should then be transferred to promising growth industries, effective demand for the products of which would be increased as a result of the successful economic development in less developed countries. Given that full employment is maintained, this sort of structural adjustment in the developed countries is the only real way to increase national incomes. Moreover, only this kind of structural adjustment in developed countries could create room for expanding exports from developing countries. Structural adjustment on both sides is required in order to achieve a 'new international division of labour' and the better utilisation of world resources.

Recently it was convincingly demonstrated by Hal B. Lary that 'the ranking of industries by factor intensities is much the same from country to country, even from the most developed to the least developed. That is to say, the phenomenon of "factor-intensity reversals" seems to be much less common, at least in manufacturing, than some other empirical studies would suggest.'[3] I also have verified the validity of the factor-proportions theorem as regards exports of manufactures (74 commodities) from the United States, Canada, Sweden, the United Kingdom, the E.E.C. and Japan.[4] These studies tend to support the conclusion that the potential for manufactured exports from less developed countries is promising, provided that a receptive and co-operative attitude is adopted by the importing countries and appropriate export-oriented industrialisation policies suited to their factor endowments are pursued by the less developed countries themselves. 'A readiness on both sides to share in the international division of labor among countries at varying levels of economic development'[5] would assure successful growth in trade from less developed to developed countries.

One of the most important consequences of the validity of the factor-proportions theorem is that trade in manufactured goods throughout the world should be liberalised. This liberalisation is necessary to maximise world productivity by providing increased opportunities for international division of labour in manufacturing industries among countries at different stages of economic development and possessing different factor endowments. This means that advanced countries should abolish the protection given to their declining labour-intensive industries as rapidly as possible, transferring the production of these goods to less developed countries. To achieve 'a new international division of labour',[6] the growth of promising manufacturing industries suited to the factor proportions of the less developed countries should be assisted by capital and technological aid and by the extension of tariff preferences.

Structural adjustment in developed countries is an essential element if new development policies are to be successful. Structural adjustment is also a key factor in the liberalisation of trade and the establishment of a free-trade area among the advanced countries. How can this structural adjustment be undertaken effectively? Strong resistance, both economic and political, can be expected. Various steps will have to be taken to assist the adjustment, along the lines of those under the United States Trade Expansion Act of 1962 and the amended Act of 1968.

There are two measures that would assist the adjustments desired. First, a fund for assisting structural adjustment should be established in every advanced country. This should become an international obligation similar to the 1 per cent of national income foreign-aid target. A certain percentage (say, one-quarter of 1 per cent) of national income could be collected through taxation for this purpose. The fund should be used for bringing about the gradual elimination of uneconomic industries and the transfer of factors of production to more productive activities where the advanced country enjoys a comparative advantage. The optimum policy would be a 'package' of subsidies to allow uncompetitive production to continue over the retirement period and of cash grants to finance the closing down of capacity. Facilities should be provided, in addition, for the retraining and movement of redundant labour.

This fund would be more efficient than direct aid to developing countries, for it could be used in the advanced countries for economic rationalisation and thus raise national welfare in their own interests. In many advanced countries, slum clearance has been widely undertaken by governments. Why should not the reclamation of uneconomic industries be undertaken also?

Secondly, some safeguards for the gradual running down of inefficient, heavily protected industries in the developed countries should be devised. A Tariff Board should be established in each developed country, or preferably as an international institution, which obliged industries to justify their claim for continued protection by tariffs and quantitative controls. Subsidies voted on an annual basis should replace tariff protection for uncompetitive production. Each year subsidised producers could be required to make out a case as to why they should continue to receive cost-reducing subsidies rather than grants designed to facilitate the running down of their productive capacity.[7]

In this way the burden of maintaining protected industries would fall on the consumers and taxpayers of the developed countries concerned rather than on the less developed countries and other exporters. Consumers in the developed countries would thus be more clearly aware of their interest in seeing uneconomic industries closed down and the harmful effects of

125

tariffs and quantitative restrictions than they seem to be at present.

Careful investigation should be made as to how best to provide aid and preferences for the purpose of facilitating structural adjustment with the least friction and greatest incentives in the advanced and less developed countries alike.

II. *Directly Productive Aid*

I have advocated closer economic integration among the Pacific-basin countries, preferably the formation of a Pacific Free Trade Area (PAFTA), but as a first step, the establishment of an Organisation for Pacific Trade and Development (OPTAD) could be useful. Trade liberalisation among the five advanced countries of the Pacific – the United States, Canada, Japan, Australia and New Zealand – would bring about a large expansion of intra-areal trade (as large as $U.S. 5,000 million or 28 per cent of intra-areal trade in 1965) which would be more significant than what can be expected through the Kennedy Round tariff reductions. Complete regional trade liberalisation would appear to have considerable advantages over partial trade liberalisation in world markets. Since another major round of global tariff reductions is not feasible within the foreseeable future, the formation of a free-trade area would seem to be an effective alternative for, and the only remaining practical road to, fostering world trade liberalisation.

Moreover, the formation of PAFTA or some such alternative is particularly desirable from the viewpoint of developing well-harmonised and efficient trade and aid policies[8] towards the less developed countries in the Pacific basin. If a PAFTA arrangement were established, the group of developed countries could (and should) offer associate membership to the less developed countries of the Pacific and provide the latter with aid, investment and trading privileges. To increase aid and trade with less developed countries, what is most needed is structural adjustment of industries in the developed countries as explained above.

The creation of PAFTA would imply that each member

126

would be prepared eventually to adjust to full competition from the other member countries. This would certainly provide developed countries with a great impetus to undertake structural reorganisation, and if this could be started, it would not be difficult to include the structural adjustments required to provide the less developed countries with wider markets. Each advanced country in isolation might be reluctant to grant aid and trading preferences to less developed countries on the scale required, either because of its lack of resources, or because it could not face alone the structural consequences for its own economy. Only harmonised and co-ordinated efforts among the advanced countries would make aid and trade expansion with less developed countries possible. The increased prosperity and higher incomes which the advanced Pacific countries would gain through PAFTA would provide them with additional resources which they could share with the less developed countries of the Pacific. Only the process of rapid economic growth within the developed countries, stimulated to some extent by trade liberalisation, makes possible structural adjustment.

Aid and trade preferences should be provided from advanced to less developed countries of the Pacific in a direction which would accelerate most the structural adjustment needed on both sides. With this aim in view, it is strongly recommended that international economic aid should be increasingly provided to Asian (and Latin American) developing countries by the advanced Pacific countries in the form of machinery, equipment, fertiliser and other capital goods for directly productive (preferably export-oriented) activities in the coming decade. Both humanitarian and infrastructural aid which were the main form of aid in the past can continue to make an important contribution in the future, but in addition to these types of aid, directly productive aid is more urgently required now. As mentioned above, it can be expected that an increase in directly productive aid will have several beneficial effects not only for the developing countries but also for the donor countries.[9]

Suppose there was an outright grant of $U.S. 1,000 million annually for the coming ten years, in addition to the current level of aid, to the Asian developing countries from the five advanced countries of the Pacific, specifically for the purpose of the importation of machinery, equipment, fertilisers and other capital goods. This would certainly stimulate the expansion of heavy and chemical industries in advanced countries, and many other indirect effects could be anticipated.

Private capital investment in the developing countries should also increase, if the capital requirements of new manufacturing industries, which need such large and risky investments that private firms sometimes hesitate to undertake the investment, are met by international grants and, in addition, if preferential treatment of their exports by the advanced countries is assured. Private capital would assist in establishing a series of ancillary, interrelated or higher-stage processing industries. For example, a big cotton-spinning mill could be established by international grants; then the weaving and clothing industries might be supplemented by foreign private as well as local capital. The mill would produce yarn cheaply, owing to low capital costs, and ancillary and interrelated industries would become profitable.

Private capital investment from advanced countries would be stimulated. Increases both in the directly productive aid and in the private capital investment would directly, and in addition the 'acceleration effect' would indirectly, create a new demand for heavy and chemical industries in the advanced countries. Moreover, the expansion of those industries would have multiplied income effects resulting in further additional demand.

A substantial expansion of heavy and chemical industries in the advanced countries could provide a stimulus large enough to reallocate resources in such a way as to expedite a rapid transfer of labour and capital (with the aid of adjustment assistance, if necessary) from agriculture and light manufactures of a labour-intensive type to heavy and chemical industries, that is, from comparatively disadvantageous to advantageous industries. Both the structural adjustments and increased national income in the advanced countries would enlarge the scope for importing certain kinds of agricultural products and light manufactures of a labour-intensive type from developing countries. Thus, if both the necessary capital goods, including technical know-how and managerial skill, and markets are provided, the expansion of export-oriented activities in the developing countries will be assured of success.

To sum up, my proposal for increasing international economic aid towards the provision of directly productive capital goods would have three distinct advantages:

(1) It would provide the developing countries with the means necessary to expand export-oriented activities.

(2) In the advanced countries, it would lead to a reallocation of resources towards heavy and chemical industries in which they possess a comparative advantage.

(3) The expansion of heavy industries, stimulated, in the advanced countries, by the increase in demand for capital goods in the developing nations, would provide the markets necessary for growing export industries in the latter. Thus, the international division of labour would move closer towards an optimum.

III. *Agricultural Development in Asian Developing Countries*

Although the expansion of the exports of manufactures suited to their abundant supply of labour is becoming the most promising path to long-term development for Asian developing countries, agricultural development is an even more urgent task in order to economise foreign exchange, to increase export earnings and to feed their people better and elevate their will to work. Pacific advanced countries (P.A.C.) should provide extensive directly productive aid to facilitate agricultural development in Asian developing countries.

A scheme for fertiliser aid

Although the countries of south and east Asia, such as India, Pakistan, Indonesia and the Republic of Korea, are agricultural countries, they suffer from severe food shortages and import foodstuffs to the approximate annual value of $U.S. 1,000 million from advanced countries in the Pacific area such as America, Australia and Canada. Although some of these imports are available in the form of American surplus agricultural aid, this is exercising a serious pressure on their already unfavourable balance of payments position. What is more, when future increases in population and per capita consumption are taken into consideration, these countries will require a large increase in production, equivalent approximately to $U.S. 3,500 million per annum, and foodstuffs to the value of approximately $U.S. 1,000 million will have to be procured in addition to the plans for increased production already tabled by the governments concerned. There is an urgent need to improve the food-producing capacity of those Asian countries in order to cover the $U.S. 2,000 million deficit in foodstuffs – the $U.S. 1,000 million already being imported from the advanced countries plus the $U.S. 1,000 million worth of additional production. The provision of chemical fertiliser aid and the construction of fertiliser factories would seem the best method of attacking this problem.

Advanced countries of the Pacific area should shift the emphasis in their agricultural assistance programmes from the provision of foodstuffs themselves to the provision of fertiliser aid. While the supply of surplus agricultural products under the American P.L.480 programme is very useful for relief in times of famine, it has made little contribution to improving agricultural productivity in South-east Asia. On the contrary, it has even tended to impair the morale of the local peasants. Fertiliser aid and the building of fertiliser factories involve much lower expenditure than assistance in foodstuffs. Today, now that America's stocks of surplus agricultural products are beginning to dry up, a switch towards emphasis on fertiliser aid would be advantageous.

A number of facts already testify that crop yields increase greatly if chemical fertilisers are applied appropriately. While production of rice per hectare is more than 4 tons in Japan, and around 3 tons in both the Republic of Korea and Taiwan, which follow Japan, in the other countries of South-east Asia yields are only about 1·2 tons per hectare, the lowest being India with 0·4 tons per hectare. The yield per hectare is clearly related to the quantities of fertiliser used, low productivity being caused by the virtual non-application of fertiliser. To take another example, of the total increase in food production of 11·2 million tons provided for under the second Indian Five-

Year Plan (1956–61), 4·6 million tons or almost half was estimated to be produced by the increased use of chemical fertilisers.

For chemical fertiliser to be used effectively, it is of course necessary that irrigation and drainage facilities should be provided in advance. Although not all South-east Asia is ready to employ fertilisers, a fairly extensive area is. Increased production should be brought about by increased use of fertilisers, beginning in the regions in which the preconditions have been established. At the same time technical advice about the use of fertilisers, insecticide and improving the seed strains should also be made available. It is an encouraging fact that superior seed strains such as IR-8 and ADT-27 have been developed and successfully used over a wide area. The diffusion of these modern agricultural inputs will take a long time and will need assiduous technical help and institutional reform, but they have already offered great hope for progress in South-east Asia.

The main features of the scheme for fertiliser aid are as follows:

(1) P.A.C. should give a gift of fertilisers to the value of $U.S. 60 million yearly, or a total value of $U.S. 300 million over a five-year period, to the countries of South-east Asia which are in a position to use them.

(2) The countries which receive these gifts of fertiliser should sell it at appropriate prices to the farmers, and should accumulate the proceeds as counterpart funds.

(3) At an appropriate time, factories for the production of fertilisers should be set up in the aid-receiving countries. When this is done, the counterpart funds should be used to pay for such local expenses as acquisition of land, local labour costs, the remuneration of P.A.C. personnel dispatched, etc. The equipment required in setting up these factories should be supplied from P.A.C. on a long-term, deferred-payment basis.

(4) The counterpart funds should be used for the following purposes in addition to the construction of fertiliser factories: (a) additional or supplementary irrigation works directly necessary for fertiliser application; (b) running expenses necessary for P.A.C.'s agricultural technical co-operation activities (experimental centres,

131

pilot or model farms, technical direction, extension work with improved strains of seed, etc.; (c) the purchase of agricultural machinery and implements, seeds, insecticide, etc.; (d) the establishment of fertiliser storage and transportation facilities.

In summary, this is an aid formula under which fertilisers (especially nitrogenous fertiliser) for which P.A.C. has a surplus productive capacity are first given as gifts, following which fertiliser factories will be built for the aid-receiving countries with the help of their counterpart funds and capital supplied under deferred-payment arrangements.

For example, if in the first year $U.S. 60 million worth of fertiliser aid were given to India and Pakistan respectively, in the second year two standard factories with a daily capacity of 600 tons of ammonium and 1,000 tons of urea could be built in each country. The cost of building one of these factories is estimated at $U.S. 25 million for the plant, and about $U.S. 15 million for local costs (to be met out of counterpart funds). In addition to this, during the second year both Indonesia and the Philippines should each be given gifts of fertilisers to the value of $U.S. 30 million. In the third year, two fertiliser factories should be built in each of these two countries. In the small countries of South-east Asia, it would, of course, be proper to make the fertiliser factories small-scale ones of half, or quarter, of the capacity of the standard factories. It would also be possible to effect exchanges among the countries receiving fertilisers and countries building factories with their counterpart funds (e.g. by exchanging fertilisers produced in India for Burmese or Thai rice), a variety of flexible applications of the scheme being conceivable.

Fertiliser aid at the rate of $U.S. 60 million yearly, or $U.S. 300 million over five years, seems modest both from the point of view of P.A.C.'s ability to meet the burden and its surplus capacity in fertiliser production. This aid alone would probably be sufficient to make up the whole of the $U.S. 2,000 million increase in food production required by South-east Asia, which was mentioned above. It is to be hoped that other advanced countries in Western Europe would also participate in the fertiliser aid scheme.

P.A.C. would not only be enabled to carry through a meaningful aid programme aimed at the solution of the most urgent problem of food shortage in the countries of South-east Asia, but the deferred-payments scheme would also enable P.A.C. to export fertiliser plants and equipment valued at as much as $U.S. 500 million over a five-year period. Once the farmers of South-east Asia became thoroughly familiar with the use of fertilisers and conscious of their value, the demand for fertilisers could be expected to increase, and even the demand for commercial exports of fertilisers from P.A.C. could be stimulated.

A programme for cash-crop plantations

There is a strong desire for industrialisation in the countries of South-east Asia, but as capital equipment imports for the purposes of industrialisation are costly, developing countries commonly fall into serious balance of payments difficulties. If, along with the above-mentioned increased food production, which reduces the demand for foreign exchange, it were possible to enlarge exports of such cash crops as raw cotton and sugar, their additional foreign exchange earnings would become available for the promotion of economic development.

There is considerable scope for the Pacific advanced countries to switch the imports of raw materials and foodstuffs from other advanced countries in the Pacific or Europe to Asian developing countries for those primary products which can be produced in Asian developing countries competitively in terms of quality, price, delivery, etc. Between five and ten years should be allowed for the developing countries to improve productivity and to increase export capacity. For advanced countries too, some time will be required for adjusting their industrial and employment structures.

The possibilities for switching sources of supply are especially great in Japan's case. Japan will have to import increasingly large quantities of raw materials, fuels and foodstuffs to sustain its expanding economy. In 1965, Japan imported two-thirds of its total consumption of energy – mostly in the form of petroleum. Japan will continue to import most of the iron ore and non-ferrous metal ores it requires.

133

Its imports of raw cotton and raw wool may decline somewhat, but Japan must continue to rely on imports for its entire consumption of these raw materials. In 1966, lumber was Japan's second-largest import, coming only after petroleum, and imports will further increase in the years to come. Imports of animal feeds such as maize and kaoliang are rapidly increasing. In 1966, Japan's fodder imports amounted to 5·7 million tons, and in the near future they will exceed the 10 million ton mark. Imports of oilseeds, sugar, bananas and marine products will also expand. If Asian developing countries can produce these products efficiently, they will be able to expand their exports to Japan greatly.[10]

For the United States, Canada, Australia and New Zealand, the possibility of increasing imports of raw materials and foodstuffs from Asian developing countries may be limited only to their traditional imports from these countries, but rapid economic growth and structural adjustments in these advanced countries will induce fairly large increases in imports from Asian developing countries for those traditional goods. It is hoped that those advanced countries are able to refrain from expanding competitive agricultural production through the abolition of support schemes and protection.

For agricultural products which Japan is importing both from the advanced countries of the Pacific area and from Southeast Asia, possible increases in Japanese imports from Southeast Asia are expected to amount to about $U.S. 700 million or $U.S. 800 million within the next five years, if one takes into account the possible trade-diversion effects away from the advanced countries and towards imports from the developing countries envisaged by our plan as well as the influence of the general increase in imports projected for Japan during this five-year period. Increased demand for Asian agricultural products in other Pacific advanced countries will be approximately the same as in Japan, making a total of roughly $U.S. 1,500 million.[11] It is desirable to have this met by increased production in South-east Asia brought about by the efficient use of directly productive aid. Although it is not easy to estimate the amount of aid required, the importation of investment goods to be used in the agricultural development projects backed by P.A.C. alone would require $U.S. 240 million. This figure is obtained from the estimates of the capital coefficient in South-east Asia (1·6) and the foreign exchange requirement rate (0·1), together with the projected total increase in demand for the agricultural products of South-east Asia of \$U.S. 1,500 million. If this sum is provided over a five-year period, about \$U.S. 50 million annually would be sufficient.

An efficient aid formula would be to grant funds and technology for the establishment and operation of cash-crop plantations. Possible cash crops to be grown on these plantations would be cotton, maize, sugar, soybeans and tobacco. Here, however, I should like to consider a plan for a cotton plantation company as a representative of such undertakings.

(1) The P.A.C. would disburse aid at an annual rate of, say, \$U.S. 30 million or a total of \$U.S. 150 million over five years in the form of technical co-operation expenses, and would set up a parent cotton plantation company. It would probably be best to entrust the running of the company's affairs to efficient private enterprise.

(2) The cotton plantation company would set up and run a number of cotton plantation joint enterprises organised with the help of local capital in suitable areas of Asia.

(3) As well as exercising control over the joint enterprises in their various locations, the parent company could provide technical assistance and would send out technicians on an organised basis. At the same time it would carry on research in marketing and technical questions of common interest, and would make joint purchases of fertilisers, machinery, agricultural implements, etc.

(4) The cotton plantation joint enterprises set up in various parts of Asia would possess the following attributes:
(a) They would have at least one primary processing factory, i.e. a factory where the seed and waste are removed by ginning machines and the selected material made up in bales, and would possess plantations sufficient in size to make possible the efficient use of the factory.
(b) They could carry out positive direction in relation to the cotton production carried on by peasant croppers in the vicinity of the plantation, buy up the raw cotton they produced, and carry out the primary processing.

135

(*c*) When a plurality of cotton plantation joint enterprises had been established in various areas in Asia, they would take steps to consider differentiating the varieties of cotton grown by the various joint enterprises in response to the needs of the demand for raw cotton in both P.A.C. and South-east Asia and with a view to distributing risks.

Japan imports most of her raw cotton from America at present, but it is quite possible from the technical point of view to grow American cotton in almost all parts of South-east Asia, and it is already being grown extensively in Pakistan. What is needed is a switch in South-east Asian cotton production to the superior variety of cotton, and to modern production management characterised by uniform quality, quality supervision, etc., and reduced costs. These should be the aims of the cotton plantation companies, and if they were achieved, not only could P.A.C.'s imports of cotton from Asian developing countries be increased, but it would also be possible to meet the demand for raw cotton which is rapidly increasing within South-east Asia itself.

It would be possible to disburse P.A.C. aid by the same method for the purpose of fostering other cash-crop plantations such as growing sugar, maize, soybeans, tobacco and other crops. All these industries would produce results quickly with comparatively little aid and contribute to the solution of Asian balance of payments problems.

Concessions, and positive support, by the advanced producing countries of the Pacific area will all be necessary to bring about the expansion of cash-crop exports from South-east Asia. The advanced countries will have to refrain from artificially stimulating their own exports, and, better still, to substitute imports from South-east Asia for domestic production. What reaction will be forthcoming from the American cotton producers is the chief worry. But it seems advisable for America to effect a gradual change-over from cotton production, which in that country is in process of losing its comparative advantage because of high wages and rising costs, to other more profitable industrial activities, and furthermore it might be more advantageous for American cotton growers to operate plantations in

South-east Asia where cheap labour is abundantly available. Thus, South-east Asia should be given an appropriate role in changing the international division of labour. Similar adjustments are required in the production of American maize and soybeans and Australian sugar.

'Fertiliser aid' and 'cash-crop plantations assistance' are two examples of aid which could be provided by the co-operative action of the Pacific advanced countries and implemented immediately, perhaps with the help of the Asian Development Bank. These directly productive aid projects should be additional to aid already planned for other purposes, since much aid is also required to equip a huge agricultural infrastructure comprising large-scale irrigation works, transport and communications facilities and education, as well as for undertaking land reform. The present scheme stresses the importance of complementary aid which allows the fruits of infrastructural aid to be realised.

The Pacific advanced countries should also assist with the development of mineral resources in Asian developing countries. This can be best done, however, mainly by private capital. Promising mineral resource developments in Asian developing countries are rather limited: iron ore in India, petroleum in Indonesia, and copper in the Philippines. The development of mineral resources in Australia, Canada and Alaska presently appears less expensive and offers more stable supplies.

IV. *PAFTA and Aid-cum-Trade Preferences*

Great faith has been put in general trade preferences to less developed countries as a means of increasing their export earnings and promoting their economic growth. Trade preferences for developing countries are justifiable if divergence from the principle of non-discrimination within GATT is temporary and if they foster liberalisation of world trade. They are positively desirable if they encourage transformation in the international division of labour in such a way as to strengthen specialisation in the export of labour-intensive products from developing countries.

137

Will the general trade preferences bring about really substantial beneficial effects to developing countries as it is hoped they will? This question was examined in the previous chapter. What my study and others have shown is that the static effects of preference schemes are not likely to be substantial. The prospects are generally discouraging for developing countries. It was suggested in the previous chapter that an aid-cum-preference scheme could offer more benefits to developing countries.

It is clear that a large-scale scheme of aid-cum-preference could be provided more efficiently and without much difficulty by a group of like-minded advanced countries. This suggests the advisability of a Free Trade Area (F.T.A.) Aid-cum-Preference System.

The optimum arrangements for the less developed countries would be for as rapid as possible a reduction of barriers on their exports to F.T.A. countries, combined with the slow and gradual elimination of barriers among F.T.A. countries. It might be best to establish an F.T.A. by eliminating tariffs gradually within ten to fifteen years, but to reduce tariffs on developing countries' products from the first year to the full extent, following on the principle of an advance-cut plan. At the same time, F.T.A. governments could increase directly productive aid and encourage the flow of private investment to developing countries which would be stimulated by these trade measures.

The F.T.A. aid-cum-preference system has a number of advantages, including greater feasibility, over the general preference system considered by UNCTAD. These have been well summarised by David Wall as follows:[12]

In the first place, the spirit behind the F.T.A. movement is based on belief in the benefits to be gained from free trade and the concessions called for in the proposed preference system would represent a more extensive diffusion of this particular spirit.

Secondly, if F.T.A. was to be successfully established, its members would be better off and consequently able to bear the cost of the preference system more easily, which contrasts with the UNCTAD scheme that incorporates no *quid pro quo* for developed countries.

Thirdly, the extension of preferences by F.T.A. as a group would ensure that the burden of accommodating those preferences would be shared as broadly as possible.

In addition, such action would reverse the tendency for the world to break up into discriminatory trading blocs bent on protecting the interests of producers within each bloc.[13]

It should be stressed again that the jolt to the economies of the developed countries which the provision of preferences to the less developed countries entails would be alleviated by the formation of F.T.A. The creation of F.T.A. implies that each member would be prepared, eventually, to adjust to full competition from other member countries. Only with such commitments would F.T.A. countries be ready to provide preferences to developing countries more widely and effectively. It is practically impossible under present world trade policies to abolish non-tariff restrictions. The abolition of non-tariff restrictions could be realised between F.T.A. members and the benefits extended to associated developing countries. Thus, the commodity coverage for reducing both tariffs and other trade barriers in favour of less developed countries would be much greater under F.T.A. preference than under the UNCTAD scheme. Tariffs and other trade barriers for less developed countries would be completely eliminated by F.T.A. preferences, while only a 50 per cent reduction of tariffs might be the largest feasible tariff cut under the UNCTAD scheme. In addition, greater assistance from F.T.A. countries would be assured. Thus, the F.T.A. aid-cum-preference system would be more beneficial to less developed countries than a general system of preferences considered by UNCTAD.

F.T.A. preferences along the lines of the advance-cut plan would automatically assure that the advantages to developing-nation exporters would last as long as the period over which F.T.A. members gradually removed barriers to trade among themselves, and also with respect to F.T.A. imports from third-party developed countries. On this point, it may appear to the less developed countries that F.T.A. preferences would be less beneficial than permanent general preferences. It should be noted, however, that any preference scheme should not be allowed to be permanent. The duration of the preference scheme should be long enough to allow the successful establishment of some industries, but not so long as to encourage the establishment of industries in which developing nations have no prospects of long-term comparative advantage.

It might be claimed by the less developed countries that the F.T.A. preference system is not general as regards countries which provide preferences, since the free-trade area is unlikely to cover all the developed countries. However, less developed countries may become associated with more than one F.T.A. and receive preferential treatment from all that were prepared to provide it. Moreover, advanced countries could belong to more than one F.T.A. This possibility arises from the characteristics of free-trade areas, which differ from customs unions or more solid political unions. If more free-trade areas provide non-discriminatory preferences to any less developed countries generally, F.T.A. preferences would really become more general and effective than those intended under the UNCTAD scheme.

V. *Conclusion*

The establishment of a Pacific Free Trade Area or an alternative organisation has the twin objectives of providing a step towards free world trade and of assisting more effectively the less developed economies, particularly in South-east Asia, in their efforts to develop. This chapter has examined how the Pacific advanced countries can co-operate to increase directly productive aid for food production, cash-crop plantations and manufacturing industries to the Asian developing countries. It has also recommended that F.T.A. preferences should be provided in close association with aid efforts.

It is worth emphasising once more that to make these aid-cum-preference efforts fruitful both for the Pacific advanced countries and Asian developing countries, three steps are necessary. Firstly, trade liberalisation among the Pacific advanced countries, preferably through the formation of a Pacific Free Trade Area, is a prerequisite for increasing their aid-giving capacity and for providing the necessary jolt to carry out structural adjustment which will allow the absorption of increased imports from developing countries. Secondly, the structural adjustment of industries in advanced countries is a key factor in the success of the entire PAFTA aid-cum-preference system. Thirdly, it goes without saying that efforts of self-help and considered policies for economic development in Asian developing countries are essential to the success of the scheme. Finally, improved financial arrangements in the Asian–Pacific region would facilitate the implementation of these trade and development policies.

6 A Pacific Currency Area: A New Approach to International Monetary Reform

I. *International Monetary Problems*

As important world traders, Pacific countries were greatly disturbed by the series of international monetary manœuvres – devaluation of sterling on 18 November 1967, the gold-rush following British devaluation and its impact on confidence in the dollar, dollar defence measures, the introduction of a two-tier gold-price system, rumours about the rearrangement of European exchange rates – that occurred during the late 1960s. These manœuvres warned of the precariousness of international economic and financial co-operation within the framework of the International Monetary Fund and the General Agreement on Tariffs and Trade, and pointed to the need for tighter international monetary and economic integration. The contribution that a Pacific Free Trade Area and Pacific Currency Area might make to the promotion of world trade liberalisation and international monetary reform should be examined with this background in mind.

In the last twenty-five years, much attention has been paid to the need for increasing international liquidity on a global basis in order to sustain rapid expansion in world trade without excessive inflation. Basically, the gold-exchange system has functioned over the years on the premise that the United States Treasury would honour its promises to buy gold from, and sell gold to, official monetary institutions in other countries at the official price ($U.S. 35 per ounce of pure gold) and has allowed the creation of additional international liquidity in so far as other countries accepted the dollar, a national currency, as a means for international transactions. However, as dollar holdings in other countries ($U.S. 15·7 billion with official monetary institutions in 1967) surpassed United States gold reserves ($U.S. 12·1 billion in the same year), confidence in the dollar dwindled. The United States was forced to reduce the deficit in her balance of payments, and thereby the creation of international liquidity through the availability of dollar reserves has been curtailed. The position in which the dollar now stands in relation to the international monetary system had an exact parallel in the case of sterling.

The International Monetary Fund has operated to create international liquidity too. Liquidity available through the I.M.F. is based upon the gold tranche which constitutes one-quarter of each member's quota allocation. The creation of international liquidity by the Fund was, however, limited by the size of members' quotas, which are fixed institutionally, and the regulations governing their use. Thus, total quotas have been increased from time to time and regulations governing drawings have been gradually softened.

In addition to these sources of liquidity, an impressive network of international credit arrangements, such as the General Agreement to Borrow, Roosa Bonds, the swap agreements between central banks and major commercial banks, has been developed partly in order to meet international monetary emergencies as they arose throughout the 1960s.

Currently, considerable faith is being placed in the creation of new international liquidity through the introduction of I.M.F. Special Drawing Rights. Seventy per cent of S.D.R.s so created will constitute a net addition to international liquidity, since they will be usable without obligation for repayment, acceptable among members, and transferable internationally.[1] This new international liquidity, it is said, should act as a third kind of international currency.

A fundamental characteristic of these international monetary institutions is that they all aim to increase international liquidity, supplementing the slow growth of monetary gold, on a global basis. But because the liquidity they create ultimately depends on the backing of monetary gold held by the United States and the I.M.F., the importance of which is diluted by the very growth of these dollar reserves, sterling reserves and I.M.F. drawings, important problems of confidence have resulted.[2]

It is said that the creation of I.M.F. Special Drawing Rights is a first step towards dethroning gold from its central position in the international monetary system. In this respect, the

143

objective of the I.M.F. reforms is similar to that of Triffin's scheme for the establishment of a world central bank.[3] Increases in international liquidity have certainly been welcomed in the past, but, significantly, only to the extent that such liquidity has been solidly backed by monetary gold holdings. When doubts about the strength of gold backing have arisen, monetary crises have occurred.[4] The demand for gold backing merely reflects the lack of international monetary integration and a parallel lack of international solidarity. A successfully managed international currency system must be founded on co-operation in an international society among like-minded countries possessing considerable solidarity in their political and economic aims. In this context, the contribution of a regional approach to the solution of the international monetary problem, paralleling the regional approach to trade liberalisation, is worth examination.

Other roads to international monetary reform have been advocated. Some economists, for example, have stressed the importance of allowing exchange rates to fluctuate more freely. These proposals for more flexible exchange rates are essentially different in their approach to the international monetary problem from the proposals for a managed international currency system. First, they aim at eliminating or reducing the need for international liquidity and emphasise rapid balance of payments adjustment through exchange revaluations, thus turning the focus from liquidity problems to adjustment problems. Second, they involve an atomistic approach in which every country engaged in foreign transactions copes independently with its own balance of payments difficulties, thus turning away from the global approach implicit in the managed-currency solution to liquidity problems.

Even if an exception is made of the extreme position taken by Friedman and Sohmen[5] in their advocacy of freely fluctuating exchange rates, these proposals appear quite unrealistic and impracticable. If there were only a limited freeing of exchange rates and they were allowed to fluctuate within a wider band (say 5 per cent) than at present,[6] or a crawling (or sliding) peg[7] allowing continual change in exchange rates were established, many disadvantages would remain. No single country can cope with large-scale speculation against its currency independently.

Even the 14·3 per cent British devaluation or the 11·1 per cent French devaluation, and the 9·3 per cent German revaluation as well, could not have been engineered successfully without consideration being taken of the possibility of retaliation and the need for financial support by other countries. Moreover, the relevant elasticities, especially for smaller and less developed countries, are likely to be so small that devaluation will be ineffective in eliminating balance of payments deficit, or devaluation will have to be so large as to be ultimately de-stabilising. Exchange-rate fluctuations make foreign trade and investment risky, and even though forward exchange arbitrage eases some of these risks, they are likely to hinder the steady growth of international trade and investment. Thus, from the businessmen's and bankers' point of view, the adjustable-peg system under the present I.M.F. arrangements is to be preferred.

There are others who advocate raising the price of gold, for example doubling it from $U.S. 35 to $U.S. 70 per ounce. This would make possible a sudden increase, from $U.S. 40 billion to $U.S. 80 billion, in international liquidity in the form of gold reserves.[8] The principal effect, it should be noted, would not come from any stimulus to gold production that resulted from the increase in the gold price, but from the revaluation of gold reserve assets.

The scheme for raising the price of gold has merit that does not attach to the alternative proposals that have been mentioned. Under alternative schemes for increasing international liquidity, there is the problem of how to deal with accumulated dollar and sterling reserves.[9] For example, if present dollar and sterling balances were converted into S.D.R.s or gold, the S.D.R. scheme and gold-exchange standard would founder. Even the flexible exchange-rate solution is made less viable because of accumulations of reserves, since they provide a source of speculative funds. If the price of gold were doubled, on the other hand, the United States and the United Kingdom could liquidate accumulated dollar and sterling balances, and the capital-gainers may be willing to provide additional aid to less developed countries.

The plan for raising the price of gold also has demerits. Quite apart from the fact that the benefits of gold revaluation would be distributed very haphazardly – indeed, in just about the least desirable fashion imaginable – and the damage that would be done to United States monetary prestige, the basic objection to this plan is that it would not provide any permanent solution to the international monetary problem. Repeated gold revaluations would be required at periodic intervals and such revaluations would be associated with a temporary excess of world liquidity and inflationary pressures. Moreover, gold revaluation would undermine confidence in the key currencies, especially in countries such as Canada and Japan which hold large dollar reserves by gentlemen's agreement with the United States.

II. *The Effect of Reserve Pooling*

The question is whether the formation of a Pacific Currency Area can buttress the international monetary system and contribute to the solution of international monetary problems. A Pacific Currency Area would possess five main characteristics. Firstly, the Pacific Currency Area suggested here would initially include the five advanced Pacific countries – the United States, Canada, Japan, Australia and New Zealand – but it would be an open-ended currency area into which other interested countries could be welcomed. Such a currency area would be established in conjunction with or prior to the formation of the Pacific Free Trade Area explained in earlier chapters.[10] Secondly, full membership would involve the pooling of gold and foreign exchange reserves. Thirdly, within the currency area, member countries would maintain fixed exchange rates in relation to the dollar, after any initial exchange adjustments that are necessary were made. In effect, therefore, the Pacific Currency Area would be a regional Dollar Area. Fourthly, in adjustments in the Area's balance of payments vis-à-vis the rest of the world, the dollar's par value in terms of gold would be allowed to fluctuate within a narrow band (say, 5 per cent above and below the par value). Limitation of these exchange fluctuations would, under normal circumstances, involve the need for exchange equalisation operations which could be effected in terms of gold. Fifthly,

146

the balance of payments among member countries could be adjusted through freer capital movement and changes in each country's credit with the reserve pool.

My proposal for the establishment of a Pacific Currency Area rests on the conviction, shared by Mundell, that

> the dollar standard that prevailed after the Second World War was an effective standard, conducive to the rapid expansion of international trade and payments and consistent with economic goals both of the United States and of the countries using the dollar as international currency and the New York market as a source of capital. A dollar standard remains the best system for a large number of countries despite the gold problem with which the United States has recently been faced. . . .[11]

The idea of a Pacific Currency Area is not unfamiliar. A number of similar schemes have been put forward, but it may be worth applying the theory of the optimum currency area to the Pacific–Asian–Latin American region and relating it specifically to the formation of a Pacific Free Trade Area.

A brief review of the theory of optimum currency areas is in order. A currency area is simply an area in which there is a common monetary unit. Ideally, perfect competition prevails in both commodity and factor markets, and prices throughout the area are equalised through competition. In other words, the common monetary unit possesses the same purchasing power over commodities and factors of production within the currency area. Finally, there is, ideally, a single monetary–fiscal authority and its monetary–fiscal policies have equivalent influence within the currency area.

This is the strict definition of an optimum currency area, which is similar to the concept of 'a country' as defined in the theory of international trade. The definition is, however, too strict and the concept as so defined too abstract. Although a single country represents an optimum currency area for all practical purposes, there will be transportation costs, and therefore some price differences, even within a single country. Moreover, one region within a single country may enjoy prosperity while others suffer recessions. And one region may have close

147

trade and investment ties with foreign countries while others may not.

The concept of a country in the theory of international trade has found an extension in the concepts of the customs union and the free-trade area. Similarly, the concept of an optimum currency area can be softened and extended. In the first place, a currency area does not necessarily require a single monetary unit but a single currency regime, or in other words, a fixed exchange-rate system with guaranteed currency convertibility. Commodities and factors of production should move much more freely within such an area and there should be greater similarity in prices and the purchasing power of currencies within it than outside. And finally, common policies with respect to the maintenance of full employment, growth, balanced international payments and stable price levels should be pursued in concert by the members of such a currency area.

Although the idea of optimality is complex and difficult to quantify precisely, a well-integrated area such as the E.E.C. or EFTA can be thought of as an optimum currency area in these terms.

An optimum currency area, either strictly or less rigidly defined, of its nature involves a form of discrimination. In trade theory, the existence of national frontiers implies some form of discrimination. The emergence of the E.E.C. and EFTA and the existence of the British Preferential Area raised the question of whether such trading arrangements contradicted the principle of non-discrimination embodied in GATT and the I.M.F. In fact, of course, their existence is admitted under Article 24 of GATT as representing progress towards freer global trade. Indeed, the free-trade area approach to trade liberalisation is justifiable on precisely the grounds that 'the free trade area is the natural arrangement for a group of countries that wish to accelerate progress towards world free trade in the face of reluctance on the part of others to adopt', and 'the free trade area method has the substantive advantage over bargaining for tariff reductions multilaterally in GATT that it promises to arrive at complete free trade, albeit only with other member countries, within a finite and predictable period of time'.[12] A similar justification is applicable to the case for the currency-

148

area approach in relation to the global approach to monetary arrangements, since the currency-area question is a direct extension and counterpart of the customs union or free-trade area argument.

Thus, an optimum currency area is a well-integrated monetary area which operates monetary–fiscal policy as if it were a single country. Firstly, within an optimum currency area there is a managed currency system and no gold reserves are required for intra-areal settlement or currency issues. Secondly, the balance of payments vis-à-vis the rest of the world is settled ultimately through gold, allowing for some fluctuation of exchange rates within a narrow band. The establishment of such currency areas would contribute to 'economising the use of gold', since gold reserve drains would be associated entirely with extra-areal deficits in the balance of payments. It can be observed how, in a parallel fashion, the use of scarce gold supplies was economised historically by a gradual shift from the public circulation of gold coin to its use as gold reserves for the banking system and then to its use as reserves by a central bank or financial authority. Thus, the formation of currency areas is not inconsistent with the pursuit of global monetary management within the framework of the gold-exchange standard, but aims to put the present system on a sounder basis. Thirdly, a successful currency area requires not only such solidarity as is required for the pursuit of co-operative internal monetary–fiscal policies, the mutual accommodation of balance of payments vis-à-vis the rest of the world, and freer commodity and capital movements, but it also implies a large degree of solidarity in political objectives. Only those countries which possess such solidarity of purpose could establish an effective currency area.

Let us examine more specifically the beneficial effects that might be derived from the formation of a Pacific Currency Area or Dollar Area. Since the Pacific Currency Area[13] would involve the pooling of gold and foreign exchange reserves, total reserves available for extra-areal settlement would increase.

(i) It can be seen that, at the end of 1967, the establishment of a Pacific Currency Area would have increased gold reserves of $U.S. 12·0 billion for the United States alone to $U.S. 13·6 billion for the area as a whole (see Table 6.1). This increase is not particularly large. It reflects the precondition, in which Canada and Japan had refrained from converting dollar reserves into gold by gentlemen's agreement. Member countries could pool reserves with the United States Federal Reserve System, but it would be preferable to establish a Pacific Reserve Bank (similar to the Bank of International Settlements at Basle). All Pacific Currency Area members, including the United States, would sell monetary gold to the Pacific Reserve Bank and deposit the receipts, on which a gold guarantee and appropriate rate of interest would be provided.

Table 6.1. Gold and Foreign Exchange Reserves of the Five Pacific Countries (at the end of 1967)

($U.S. million)

	Gold	Reserve Position in I.M.F.	Foreign exchanges	Total international reserves
United States	12,060	420	2,340	14,830
Other four countries	1,585	877	3,840	6,302
Canada	1,015	433	1,260	2,709
Japan	338	239	1,453	2,030
Australia	231	205	993	1,429
New Zealand	1	–	134	134
Total	13,645	1,297	6,180	21,132

Source: I.M.F., *International Financial Statistics.*

(ii) At the end of 1967, the I.M.F. reserve position was $U.S. 420 million for the United States and $U.S. 877 million for the other four countries, amounting to $U.S. 1,300 million for the area as a whole. If members agreed to use I.M.F. reserves through a pooling agreement, the maximum availability of credit through the I.M.F. for the Pacific Currency Area as a whole would be substantial.

(iii) Foreign exchange reserves at the end of 1967 amounted to $U.S. 2·34 billion for the United States and $U.S. 3·84 billion for the other four countries, or $U.S. 6·2 billion for the

150

Pacific Currency Area as a whole. The foreign exchange reserves of Canada ($U.S. 1·26 billion) and Japan ($U.S. 1·45 billion)[14] were mainly dollar reserves, whilst those of Australia ($U.S. 1·0 billion) and New Zealand ($U.S. 0·13 billion) were mainly sterling. United States reserves comprised the currencies of various countries. Thus, foreign exchange reserves for extra-areal payments, other than in sterling, would not be large for the area as a whole. As mentioned before, more than anything else, this reflects the precondition necessary to the establishment of the currency area, which would have the effect of putting existing gentlemen's agreements on a sounder institutional footing.

Table 6.2. Bilateral Relationships between Changes in Reserves, 1955–67

	Australia	Canada	Japan	New Zealand	United States
Australia	*·264*	·138	− ·380	·189	·294
Canada	·006	*·163*	− ·019	·323	− ·378
Japan	− ·030	− ·001	*·296*	·274	− ·667
New Zealand	·002	·002	·006	*·039*	− ·412
United States	·120	− ·084	− ·269	− ·022	*1·361*

Note: Entries above diagonal are correlation coefficients (r_{ij}), entries along the diagonal are standard deviations (σ_i in billions of U.S. dollars), and entries below the diagonal are covariances $(r_{ij}\, \sigma_i\, \sigma_j)$.
Source of original data: *International Financial Statistics*.

The second benefit of forming a Pacific Currency Area would derive from economy in the pooling of reserves by the group of countries as a whole. Richard N. Cooper presented an interesting model for assessing the extent to which reserves could be economised through reserve pooling.[15] This study covered the period 1955–66, but here the period covered extends from 1955 to 1967.

In Table 6.2, the standard deviation of year-to-year reserve changes in billions of U.S. dollars for each country is shown on the main diagonal. The sum of the standard deviations for all five countries amounts to $U.S. 2,123 million, which represents the minimum reserve requirements for the separate settlement of occasional deficits in their international payments under the assumption that the amount of reserves required to meet these contingencies is directly related to the expected size of the contingencies, that is, the expected standard deviation of disturbances in the balance of payments.

It is usual that when the payments position of the United States deteriorates, that of Japan or Canada tends to improve, and vice versa. Generally this relationship between balance of payments positions will be more usual, the closer are ties of trade and capital between two countries. When this relationship exists, the pooled reserves of a pair of countries are less liable to change than are the reserves of each country separately. The entries above the diagonal in Table 6.2 record the correlation coefficients for reserve changes of each relevant pair of countries. Gains from reserve pooling arise for any degree of correlation less than unity, but the gains increase as the correlation falls, and the maximum gains are obtained when the correlation is minus unity. The correlation between the United States and Japan (-0.67) was the highest negative correlation recorded for the period; next was that between the United States and New Zealand (-0.41); and the correlations between Japan and Australia, and the United States and Canada (both of which were -0.38), were also negatively high. Thus, it is clear that large absolute gains would have arisen from pooling reserves between these pairs of countries during the period in question.

The absolute gains from reserve pooling are indicated by the covariances, that is, the product of each correlation coefficient with the two relevant standard deviations, in the entries recorded below the diagonal in Table 6.2. The standard deviation of combined reserve changes for the five Pacific countries[16] would have been $U.S. 1,250 million, compared with the sum of standard deviations for the countries taken separately, which amounted to $U.S. 2,123 million. Hence, the pooling of reserves would have reduced the need to hold reserves against contingent payments deficits by 41 per cent.[17] 'This could represent a substantial saving, and if the experience of the past decade is any guide to the future, it suggests that reserve pooling might be mutually beneficial.'[18]

III. *The Effectiveness of Floating Exchange Rates*

I have suggested that in the adjustment of extra-areal payments, exchange rates should be allowed to float within a small band (say, 5 per cent above and below par value) and that this measure be supplemented by exchange equalisation operations when necessary. Another way of putting this would be to say that the margins on the United States buying price and selling price for gold should be widened by 5 per cent either side of par value. As Mundell has suggested, such a proposal is quite consistent with the gold-pegging clauses in the I.M.F.[19] The effects of this means of adjustment in extra-areal payments for a Pacific Currency Area should be examined in more detail.

Why would more flexible exchange rates be effective for a Pacific, or any such large, currency area, in view of our judgement that they would not be workable for a single country? Significantly, for a large currency area like a Pacific Currency Area, the relevant balance of payments elasticities would be larger than for a single country. In consequence, relatively large gaps in such a currency area's extra-areal balance of payments would be more readily adjusted through small changes in exchange rates (or gold margins). There are three main reasons for this.

First, it can be expected that the price elasticity of import demand would be larger for the Pacific Currency Area as a whole than for each separate member country. Since imports are the excess of domestic demand over domestic production, the price elasticity of import demand, η, is shown by:

$$\eta = \theta \left(\frac{P}{M} e + \frac{C}{M} d \right),$$

where θ is the elasticity of domestic prices with respect to changes in the price of competitive imports, and takes a constant value which depends upon the degree of product and quality differentiation between domestic and imported goods, the tastes of consumers, and policies such as buy-national-product policies; e and d are the price elasticity of demand and supply respectively; and P/M and C/M are the ratios of domestic

153

production and consumption to imports respectively (where $C = P + M$). Since θ, e and d are constant for each commodity, the smaller the degree of import dependence, or the larger P/M and C/M, the larger will be η, the price elasticity of import demand.

The formation of a free-trade area or an optimum currency area among a group of countries shifts some proportion of each member country's imports into areal production, since some proportion of each member country's trade will be with partner countries. Thus, it is obvious that the ratio of production to imports for the area as a whole will be larger than for each member country separately.

The more intensive intra-areal trade, the larger will be the ratio of production to imports for the area as a whole relative to the similar ratio for each participating country. The ratio of intra-areal trade to world trade for the five Pacific countries concerned was 32·5 per cent in 1958; this had increased to 37·3 per cent in 1965, which compares well with the share of 43·5 per cent for intra-areal trade among the E.E.C. countries.

The results will not only be affected by the aggregate ratio of intra-areal trade to total trade, but also by the composition of member countries' imports and exports. Take, for example, the case of a member country whose imports consist mainly of raw materials which are not produced within the area, and whose supplies are all obtained from outside the area. The areal ratio of production to imports will not increase for those products with the formation of a currency area. In other words, the key to effective operation of the exchange mechanism in this context is the extent of substitutability between areal and outside production. In this respect, the formation of a Pacific Currency Area, which would include not only exporters of manufactures, such as Japan and the United States, but also major primary producers such as Australia and New Zealand, and the diversified Canadian economy, recommends itself. Within that region there is likely to be a high degree of substitutability with respect to outside supplies, and aggregate elasticities of import demand for outside commodities are likely to be high – much more so, for example, than for the E.E.C.

It can be demonstrated, by the so-called stability condition for the balance of payments,[20] that the greater the elasticity of import demand, the more effective small changes in exchange rates will be in adjusting imbalance in the balance of payments.[21]

Secondly, the formation of a Pacific Currency Area, if accompanied by progress towards a free-trade area, would be associated with the growth of intra-areal trade stimulated by the trade-creation, trade-diversion and dynamic effects of such trade liberalisation. Trade dependence on the outside world would decrease relative to growing intra-areal trade dependence, and the increased price elasticities of import demand would buttress the effectiveness of more flexible exchange rates vis-à-vis the rest of the world.

The third reason why flexible exchange rates are likely to be more effective for a currency area than for a single country relates to the importance of 'money illusion'. Exchange fluctuations are more fully effective in so far as consumers in the devaluing country resist downward movements in wages and prices expressed in terms of domestic currency but do not resist the same real changes if these are effected by changes in exchange rates. In other words, the argument for flexible exchange rates rests on the proposition that money wages in domestic currency are inflexible, but that real wages are not inflexible if they are changed by alteration of the exchange rate. In a country which imports all of its foodstuffs and exports all of its output, an alteration of the exchange rate would lead to an immediate and proportionate change in the cost of living, and one can assume that the real effects of these changes would be noticed. On the other hand, if a country imports a very small proportion of its consumption, one would expect that an exchange-rate alteration would have no perceptible influence on the cost of living, at least in the short run, and would not lead to any general upward movement in wages and prices. Hence, it is reasonable to expect that the larger the optimum currency area and the smaller its dependence on extra-areal trade, the more effective flexible exchange rates are likely to be.[22]

These three factors suggest that flexible exchanges would present an effective means whereby a Pacific Currency Area could adjust its balance of payments vis-à-vis the rest of the world. The only significant problems would arise through speculative attacks upon the dollar, the currency area's key currency. But to meet that problem, exchange equalisation

operations with total reserves of $U.S. 21·1 billion or gold and
I.M.F. reserves of $U.S. 15·0 billion would not seem inadequate.

IV. *Intra-areal Balance of Payments Adjustment*

Countries hold international reserves, if possible the optimum
amount of reserves, so that they can be used as a buffer against
the adverse effects of short-term balance of payments variations on important economic policy objectives, such as the
pursuit of long-run economic growth, the maintenance of full
employment, and stability in the domestic price level. A large
currency area will hold reserves for the same reasons. Such a
currency area will be the more effective if its reserve pool is
large, there is scope for economising reserves, and flexible
exchange rates work efficiently to adjust the extra-areal
balance of payments. A Pacific Currency Area is desirable
specifically because it will help to free the pursuit of these
important economic objectives from short-run balance of
payments considerations.

The establishment of a Pacific Currency Area would have
several important effects on the efficiency with which intra-
areal settlements are made. In the first place, the cost of
exchange transactions would be reduced, since within the
currency area fixed exchange rates would be maintained between member-country currencies. More particularly, Japan
presently settles most of her foreign exchange transactions
through the United States dollar, while Australia and New
Zealand settle most of their accounts through sterling. In the
settlement of transactions between, say, Japan and Australia,
three clearing operations are required: between Japanese yen
and the United States dollar, between the Australian dollar and
sterling; and between the dollar and sterling in London or
New York. Each clearing demands the payment of some com-
mission. Moreover, the relevant exchange rates fluctuate, even
within the small margin of $\frac{3}{4}$ per cent, and the accumulated
margin in three clearing operations is not insignificant in
businessmen's profit calculations. These extra costs would be
eliminated if a foreign exchange market were organised with a

156

Pacific Currency Area so as to allow direct clearing between the Japanese yen and Australian dollar or between any pair of member-country currencies. It might also be feasible to eliminate the marginal fluctuations of member-country exchange rates around their par values, and implement a rigid fixed exchange-rate system within the currency area.

There are differences of view about the most efficient means of adjustment in the balance of payments between the member countries of an optimum currency area. James Meade argues that a common market or optimum currency area can work effectively only if there are flexible exchange rates between the member countries, since a common market eliminates tariffs and import restrictions and exposes countries to much more competitive and international pressure.[23] Mundell and McKinnon, on the other hand, argue that a common currency or fixed exchange-rate system is necessary for a currency area to work effectively.[24] Only under these conditions, they assert, can there be full integration and the free movement of factors. Indeed, if capital is sufficiently mobile, balance of payments gaps will be filled and flexible exchange rates become unnecessary, perhaps positively harmful.[25]

The answer to this question really turns on the extent of factor mobility, especially capital mobility, that prevails after the establishment of the currency area. In a Pacific Currency Area, the nature of payments flows, and the strength of pooled reserves, suggest that short-term capital would flow rapidly and freely enough to accommodate balance of payments fluctuations.

While a floating exchange rate makes the integration of securities markets among countries very difficult, a fixed exchange-rate system facilitates both this and the movement of capital. Perhaps a 'free-investment area' could be established in conjunction with a free-trade area in the Pacific region.[26] The practical importance of this notion arises out of the interest of American business, supported by the United States Government, in direct investment overseas. In fact, there would be mutual gains from the liberalisation of capital movement within the Pacific area, although there are some major obstacles to its attainment. First, the United States balance of payments position imposes constraints on capital outflow. Second, there is

157

reluctance bordering on fear of free capital inflow in Japan. Japan would be wise to adopt a more positive attitude towards capital inflow. It is likely to do this rapidly as Japanese business begins to overcome its inferiority complex vis-à-vis American business, and as the heavy industrial sector in Japan strengthens its competitive position and learns from experience how to handle direct foreign competition.

The mobility of capital depends upon stability in the value of currencies, which in turn depends upon sound monetary–fiscal policy within each country, under a managed-currency system with fixed intra-areal exchange rates. Since the optimum currency area as a whole operates as a managed-currency system, the stability of currencies within the area as a whole, and each member country individually, depends upon the pursuit of effective incomes policies which hold increases in money wages in line with increases in productivity. More long-term capital will flow to members who are successful in the pursuit of sound incomes policies, and will act to stimulate more rapid growth in those countries.

Within a Pacific Currency Area, adjustments in the balance of payments between member countries should rely upon sound monetary–fiscal policies and the improvement of productivity in the long run, supplemented by short-run accommodation from pooled reserves and short-term capital movements. As is the case within the framework of the present adjustable-peg system, this would not prevent the rearrangement of par values among member-country currencies should fundamental balance of payments disequilibria appear.

V. The Effect on Economic Development

The formation of an optimum currency area, such as that proposed for Pacific countries, has discriminatory effects. Member countries maintain fixed exchange rates and have arrangements for accommodating payments among themselves, but exchange rates are allowed to fluctuate vis-à-vis the rest of the world. The establishment of a Pacific Currency Area would be accompanied by the creation of a free-trade area and free-investment area, both of which would have favourable effects on investment flows within the area. But since the mobility of capital between different regions depends in part on stability in the value of currencies between them, floating exchange rates vis-à-vis the outside world would tend to discriminate against extra-areal investment flows. In fact, there would be investment creation, both in consequence of stabilising payments arrangements within the currency area and in consequence of any intra-areal trade liberalisation, and 'investment diversion' both in consequence of floating exchange rates vis-à-vis the outside world and in consequence of the discriminatory removal of trade barriers.[27] The elimination of trade barriers would induce enterprise to expand trade as well as investment within the area.[28] In this context, investment should be thought of not only, or even primarily, in terms of pure capital flows, that is, a shift of real resources from one country to another, but also in terms of the transfer of management skill and technical know-how.

Neighbouring less developed countries in Asia and Latin America would almost certainly become interested in a Pacific Currency Area, and this should be welcomed. In that case, the original members of the currency area could co-operate in the business of 'aid creation', usefully associated with 'investment creation', in the wider Pacific region, and contribute significantly to its economic development.

To date, the United States has tended to look towards the possibility of ultimately 'going in with Europe', and has tended to neglect the Pacific region. The flow of financial reserves and direct investment from America to Pacific countries has lagged behind that going to Europe. The Pacific, Asian and Latin American region has a huge potential for trade growth and development compared with Europe, and this potential should be cultivated through the formation of a Pacific Currency Area and PAFTA.

Balance of payments difficulties in America, especially since about 1958, have led to increased restraint on overseas investment, although important exceptions have been made in the Pacific area and for less developed countries, and to reduced aid coupled with increasingly 'tied' aid.[29] 'Tied' aid, it hardly needs saying, is frequently less economic than 'untied' aid,

since it often obliges the recipient country to receive uncompetitive or unwanted products which are available much
more cheaply from other sources of supply than the donor
country.[30]

A prime task is to devise an effective international mechanism
which allows donor countries, such as the United States,
to increase aid and investment in the Pacific–Asian–Latin
American region and 'untie' development loans without in-
curring balance of payments difficulties and a drain on gold
reserves. A few years back, I suggested that this might be
managed through a 'Lent Currency Scheme',[31] the essentials
of which can be implemented more conveniently through an
extended Pacific Currency Area.

The premise upon which my earlier proposal was based was
that a major element in balance of payments disturbances was
the leakage from grants, loans and military expenditures
granted by one country to another but spent in a third country.
This is the familiar transfer problem that dogged German
reparations after the First World War and that has, in a sense,
been the root cause of the American balance of payments
difficulties in recent years. Even if one assumes, given the tying
of loans that has been common, that only 20 per cent of private
capital outflows, government grants and military expenditures
were spent in third countries, this leakage would itself account
for the major part of America's large net monetary deficit,
resulting in the drainage of gold. My proposal is aimed at
bridging these transfer difficulties.

The Pacific Reserve Bank, proposed above, could also assume
the functions of a development bank, or become the Pacific
Reserve and Development Bank. The institutional arrangements necessary to these proposals would be as follows:

(1) When member country A from the Pacific Currency
Area provides country B with long-term private investment or
aid funds (in the form of grants, loans, etc.), country B deposits
20 per cent of the borrowed amount with P.R.D.B. This may
be called 'Lent "A" Currency' (that is, Lent Dollars, Lent
Yen, etc.).

(2) The Lent Currency is exchangeable with an equivalent
to any convertible national currency, and one kind of Lent
Currency (say, Lent Dollars) can be exchanged for another (say,

Lent Yen). It is not, however, convertible into gold. This prevents a drain of gold from lending countries. The gold guarantee is assured for Lent Currency.

(3) The Lent Currency, once deposited by the borrowing country, is used for payment to any country when the borrowing country imports goods and services.

(4) The borrowing country, B, is able to use currency thus acquired to make purchases from any country, even from outside the Currency Area, provided that the country, D, joins in the Pacific Currency Area Lent Currency scheme and is therefore willing to accept Lent Currency. Thus P.C.A. would be an open-ended currency area.

(5) The Lent Currency circulates in the Pacific Currency Area market as do other convertible national currencies, and ultimately falls into the hands of a balance of payments surplus country (called country C) or will be deposited by such a country with P.R.D.B. (When country A – the lending country – earns a balance of payments surplus, the Lent 'A' Currency is cleared automatically. There is no transfer difficulty.) This means that country C, who is the net earner of international liquidity owing to country A's lending to country B, has to refrain from converting earned Lent Currency into gold, and, instead, has to provide short-term credits by holding Lent Currency within the Pacific Currency Area. Thus, international liquidity within P.C.A. will be augmented in the form of Lent Currency.

(6) A favourable rate of interest should be payable on Lent Currency deposited with P.R.D.B. The rate of interest should be a little higher than that which is obtainable from the holding of other international liquidity. This arrangement would make the deposit of Lent Currency with P.R.D.B. more attractive than the holding of other international liquidity and would stimulate a gradual shift from the latter to the former.

(7) Other transfer difficulties are associated with the repayment of loans by the borrowing country B to the lending country A. Under normal circumstances, the Lent 'A' Currency will be cleared in such a way that country B earns a balance of payments surplus and receives Lent 'A' Currency and repays it to country A. Hence, country A does not sustain a balance of payments deficit, which usually requires additional adjustment,

by the amount of the return flow. Lent Currency efficiently fulfils its purpose in bridging, through time, the two transfer difficulties accompanying the lending and repaying of long-term capital and aid transactions.

(8) If the third country, C, earns a balance of payments surplus in the course of the return flow, transfer difficulties also result. Country C should reduce its surplus and liquidate accumulated Lent 'A' Currency. However, if country C maintains its balance of payments surplus, it will accumulate more Lent Currency and it can continue to accumulate Lent Currency just so long as it wishes, providing more credit in that form at its own risk. If country C does not want to accumulate more Lent Currency, it will have to adjust its balance of payments out of surplus, either by increasing its own foreign investment and aid or by domestic expansionary policies which increase imports. Thus, reluctance to hold Lent Currency stimulates an automatic adjustment mechanism in the balance of payments which is built into this proposal.

If this scheme works successfully,[32] it is clear that wealthier countries, especially the United States, would increase the investment and aid they extend to Pacific Currency Area countries, without having to worry about excessive balance of payments strain and the gold drain. Moreover, the advanced countries within the Pacific Currency Area would be able to provide more aid to neighbouring less developed countries without having to 'tie' aid individually, although in practice they would be 'tying' aid as a group to some extent. Less 'tied' aid would almost certainly enhance the efficiency of aid.[33]

VI. *Feasibility of a Pacific Currency Area*

The desirability of a wide optimum currency area which adopted flexible exchange rates vis-à-vis the rest of the world was first suggested in 1963 in the Brookings Report.[34] International monetary disturbances since then, as I have suggested above, give added emphasis to the need for such an arrangement for promoting closer international monetary co-operation in the Pacific region. Business circles recently took the initiative in

162

establishing the Private Investment Company for Asia, capitalised with $U.S. 40 million in March 1969. The Pacific Free Trade Area and Currency Area schemes have the twin aims of promoting free trade among the five advanced Pacific countries and of expanding aid and trade growth between those advanced countries and neighbouring less developed countries. The establishment of PICA is consistent with these aims.

The establishment of a Pacific Currency Area depends largely on the attitude taken by the United States. Canada is already a *de facto* member of the Dollar Area. Japan also holds dollars and refrains from converting them into gold under a gentlemen's agreement with the United States. Australia has moved rapidly and increasingly into the Pacific financial network. New Zealand, whose ties with the Sterling Area are strongest, is also gradually changing her attitude towards the region. The pooling of gold and foreign exchange reserves would represent a sounder institutionalisation of growing financial co-operation in the Pacific region.

The international credit network among the five advanced Pacific countries is already well developed. Japan, Canada and Australia rely heavily upon United States capital. Although capital imports do not provide a very large proportion of their domestic capital formation, the contribution is hardly marginal. The Interest Equalisation Tax on United States purchases of foreign securities and a 'voluntary credit restraint program' applicable to foreign lending by American banks were recently introduced because of the United States balance of payments difficulties, although a partial exemption from these measures was accorded the Pacific region. There has also been co-operation in the provision of loan funds through the Asian Development Bank.[35] The establishment of a Pacific Reserve and Development Bank which promoted economic development in the Pacific–Asian–Latin American region through increased aid and investment would be a further step in the same direction. A regional code of overseas investment and aid could also be adopted if it seemed desirable.

One question that arises is whether P.C.A.'s establishment presupposes the establishment or strengthening of other currency areas, such as a European Currency Area, the Sterling Area and the Rouble Area, at the same time.[36] I believe that the establishment of a Pacific Currency Area can be proceeded with independently of the establishment or strengthening of other currency areas. Even a single country represents one optimum currency area. Though the arguments presented here for the establishment of P.C.A. apply to other areas, they should decide what is best in their own political and economic interests.

The position of sterling and the Sterling Area is another matter. Should Britain join a Dollar Area or a European Currency Area? Should the Sterling Area attempt to strengthen itself independently? The currency-area alternatives for Britain are similar to the free-trade area alternatives.

If P.C.A. were established, it would be better if the United States did not raise the price of gold, since a large share of dollar balances is held by P.C.A. countries. The problem becomes how much of the dollar balances held by the rest of the world would seek gold conversion. Triffin has estimated that excessive dollar holdings in the E.E.C. stood at $U.S. 3·65 billion at the end of September 1966.[37] Even though this account will have risen since 1966, only some part of it would seek conversion, and P.C.A.'s pooled reserves and flexible exchange rates vis-à-vis the outside world should be adequate to cope with the contingency.

The prospects for both a Pacific Currency Area and PAFTA depend largely on United States attitudes. The proposals outlined above represent an outward-looking, non-isolationist alternative for the new United States Administration.

7 PAFTA as a New Design for World Trade Expansion

I. *Closer Pacific Trade Partnership*

The principal themes of this book can be summarised briefly. Stresses within the world trading system since the conclusion of the Kennedy Round of tariff reductions (June 1967) and within the international monetary system, particularly since the devaluation of sterling (November 1967), suggest that there is need for a new design for further trade liberalisation and fostering the continued expansion of world trade as well as for stabilisation of the world monetary system. At the same time, developing countries throughout expect more aid and assistance with trade expansion through the extension of general trade preferences. Rigid adherence to multilateral and non-discriminatory free-trade principles seems a questionable guideline, and it might well be more sensible to seek the benefits of trade expansion through a regional or free-trade area approach to trade liberalisation. The E.E.C. and EFTA both suggest the effectiveness of the regional approach to trade liberalisation. Recently, the formation of a North Atlantic Free Trade Area has been strongly advocated.[1] Why should the five Pacific countries, the United States, Canada, Japan, Australia and New Zealand, not prepare for the formation of a Pacific Free Trade Area and welcome British participation? Could not PAFTA and NAFTA be linked through common United States–Canadian participation?

The Pacific ranks alongside Western Europe as one of the two major centres of world trade. Trade among the five advanced Pacific countries, the United States, Canada, Japan, Australia and New Zealand, increased by 97 per cent between 1958 and 1965, from \$U.S. 9·16 billion to \$U.S. 18·02 billion, and their share in world trade rose from 7·99 per cent to 10·38 per cent. Trade within the E.E.C. grew from \$U.S. 6·86 billion to \$U.S. 20·84 billion over the same period.

Furthermore, mutual trade among advanced Pacific countries has intensified over the years. Intra-areal trade constituted 32·5 per cent of total Pacific country trade in 1958, but 37·3 per cent in 1965. In contrast, intra-areal trade was 30·1 per cent of total E.E.C. trade in 1958 and 43·5 per cent in 1965.

The formation of a Pacific Free Trade Area would, in fact, bring about a comprehensive trade liberalisation among participating countries, with the elimination of tariffs on a substantial proportion of their commodity trade. The impact effect of Pacific tariff elimination would be to increase trade by $U.S. 5,000 million. This represents an expansion of 28 per cent on intra-areal trade, or 10·3 per cent on Pacific country exports to, and 11·9 per cent on imports from, the whole world. In other words, there would be significant trade expansion, a far greater trade expansion than can be expected under Kennedy Round tariff reductions. Kennedy Round tariff reductions will probably only lead to a 5·5 per cent increase in exports and a 7·7 per cent increase in imports.

Complete regional trade liberalisation would appear to have considerable advantages over partial trade liberalisation in world markets. This is especially true if, as is most probable, another major round of global tariff reductions is not feasible within the next ten or twenty years. In that event, the formation of PAFTA would seem an effective alternative for mutual trade expansion among the five advanced Pacific countries.

At this stage, however, the PAFTA proposal seems premature, unless there is some further unforeseen disturbance in the free-world economy. It is as yet neither economically nor politically feasible. Firstly, American interests are presently world-wide and the United States could not participate readily either in a Pacific or in a European regional grouping. For the moment the United States appears committed to a global non-discriminatory approach to freer trade.[2]

Secondly, the five Pacific countries still lack the solidarity and degree of integration that would be necessary for dispensing with protective measures for the main sectors of their economies involved in regional trade – the labour-intensive industries in some countries, the agricultural and pastoral industries in other countries.[3]

Thirdly, the static gains from complete trade liberalisation

166

would differ widely from one country to another because of the disparity in stages of industrialisation within the region.

However, the realisation of PAFTA might be precipitated by a shock which came from outside the area. Greater European integration between the E.E.C. and EFTA could produce an 'inward-looking' Europe, whereupon the United States might well find closer integration in the Pacific desirable and necessary. Should the United Kingdom fail again to join the E.E.C., she might probe the establishment of a North Atlantic Free Trade Area with the United States and Canada. In that case, Japan, Australia and New Zealand would have to consider seriously steps towards closer integration within the region.

Economic integration in the Pacific should take the form of a free-trade area rather than a customs union or political union. A free-trade area arrangement would have advantages over the alternatives from several points of view: it is consistent with the rules of the General Agreement on Tariffs and Trade; it preserves the autonomy of members with respect to their tariff policies vis-à-vis non-participants; and it is a purely commercial arrangement, carrying no obligation for eventual political federation or union.[4]

Whether or not a free-trade area can ultimately be established, the five advanced Pacific countries should now set about establishing closer and more profitable trade partnerships with each other. To date, the United States has tended to look towards the possibility of ultimately 'going in with Europe', and has tended to neglect the Pacific region. The flow of financial resources and direct investment from America to Pacific-basin countries, including Asian and Latin American countries, has lagged behind that going to Europe. The Pacific, Asian and Latin American region has a huge potential for trade growth and development compared with Europe, and it should be looked at more closely.

Studies of, and proposals for, Pacific trade expansion have been quite limited. However, movement in this direction has recently been initiated. The Canada–United States Automotive Agreement took effect from January 1965. This should be given much attention as a pioneer project in selective industrial integration.[5] The Australia–New Zealand Free Trade Agreement was initiated in January 1966.[6] The Pacific Basin Economic Co-operation Committee was established among business circles in the five Pacific countries in April 1967; and a number of bilateral co-operative activities have also been promoted within business circles. It is also worth noting that Mr Takeo Miki, Japan's former Foreign Minister, and Mr Kiichi Miyazawa, former Minister of the Economic Planning Agency, are keenly interested in promoting economic co-operation in the Pacific and Asian region. Academic circles have also begun hard to probe the foundations for economic integration in this region.[7]

Before the establishment of PAFTA, several steps towards closer Pacific economic co-operation might be practicable immediately. Five main objectives suggest themselves:

(1) To increase the flow of financial resources from the United States to other Pacific countries, as well as to Asian and Latin American developing countries.

(2) To stimulate horizontal trade among the five advanced Pacific countries in heavy manufactures and chemicals and to expand production and trade of raw materials and intermediate goods more efficiently for the region as a whole.

(3) To readjust production and trade in agricultural commodities among the five Pacific countries, taking into consideration their relationship with Asian and Latin American developing countries.

(4) To readjust production and trade in light manufactures, which are labour-intensive, with the aim of providing greater access for Asian and Latin American countries in advanced-country markets.

(5) To co-ordinate the aid policy of the five advanced Pacific countries towards Asian and Latin American developing countries.

Practical steps towards closer Pacific economic co-operation can be taken by strengthening *functional*, rather than *institutional*, integration, and thus attempting to attain the favourable benefits of a free-trade area whilst avoiding the unfavourable impact effects. To realise these objectives, I suggest the initiation of three codes of international behaviour and the formation of two new regional institutions.

(1) *A code of good conduct* in the field of trade policy, under which countries would relinquish the right to raise tariffs or impose other forms of trade restriction,[8] and would gradually reduce those trade barriers particularly on the import of agricultural products and labour-intensive light manufactures, should be promulgated.

(2) *A code of overseas investment* to promote mutual investment among the five advanced Pacific countries, most effectively from the United States, and to foster the activity of joint ventures is much needed to promote trade expansion, especially horizontal trade expansion in heavy manufactures,[9] and for the development of the vast mineral resources of the Pacific region. A code which minimises the fear of American capital domination and maximises protection for America's balance of payments would greatly facilitate overseas investment and the better allocation of regional resources.

(3) *A code of aid and trade policies towards associated developing countries* is also required, so that Asian and Latin American countries might enjoy the benefits of larger markets for their agricultural products and light manufactures. The flow of developmental aid must be increased, appropriate aid projects selected, and domestic industrial structures adjusted to meet the legitimate trade needs of affiliated less developed countries.

An Organisation for Pacific Trade and Development (OPTAD) should be established in order to give effect to these codes of international behaviour. Its main features would be similar to those of the O.E.C.D., and it could be structured in the same way, with three committees on trade, investment and aid.[10]

Further, a Pacific Currency Area and Pacific Reserve and Development Bank would be established with the aim of strengthening the international monetary system and facilitating economic development within the Pacific, Asian and Latin American region.

II. *Options for the Pacific*

The best choice for Japan is to expand and free mutual trade with every trading region. The present stage of her industrialisation, her dual pattern of trade with developed and developing countries, and her geographical location dictate such a choice. However, if a further global tariff reduction is not likely to be feasible in the near future and if, moreover, the compartmentalisation of world trade is promoted further, a serious concern for Japan would be to devise measures for expanding trade on an assured basis through establishing the Pacific Free Trade Area or some such alternative.

The establishment of PAFTA would bring the largest static gains to Japan among the five Pacific countries. Japan's exports would increase by $U.S. 1,740 million or 20·6 per cent of her total exports, and her balance of trade with the area would improve by $U.S. 1,310 million, based upon the 1965 trade figures. These gains would be far greater than in the case of global tariff reductions on the scale undertaking through the Kennedy Round: these are likely to increase Japan's exports by a mere 8·8 per cent.

The big gains for Japan from the establishment of PAFTA derive, firstly, from the fact that Japan's exports depend as much as 37 per cent upon the PAFTA markets. Compared with other PAFTA countries, European markets are not so important (13 per cent) for Japan.

Secondly, about 95 per cent of Japan's exports to other Pacific countries are manufactures, which would enjoy a greater expansion from trade liberalisation, while about 71 per cent of Japan's imports are primary products, which would not increase very much in consequence of tariff reductions.

When the time comes for Japan to consider economic integration, a Pacific Free Trade Area would certainly be her best choice. Japan is destined by geography to participate in political arrangements in the Pacific rather than in Europe. On the other hand, economic integration without the United States, which holds a 30 per cent share in Japan's trade, would appear a less attractive choice.

Thus, Japan would benefit from the establishment of PAFTA, or from some other alternative, through the cheaper

170

import of raw materials and other primary products, the expansion of her exports of light manufactures, and the promotion of horizontal trade in heavy manufactures and chemicals.

The formation of PAFTA or some other alternative for economic co-operation among the five Pacific countries is desirable for Japan for another reason. Collective measures by Pacific countries are especially desirable for assisting economic development and trade growth in South-east Asian countries.

Asian markets are very important for Japan even relative to other Pacific advanced countries. The share of Asia (excluding mainland China) in Japan's total exports remains as large as 28 per cent, though it has been decreasing. Japan cannot disregard the interests of developing countries, especially in South and South-east Asia, and the same applies to the United States vis-à-vis Latin America. The question is often raised: should Japan rely on the rapidly increasing but competitive markets in developed countries, or on the complementary but more slowly expanding markets in developing countries? She has, we have stressed, to expand trade in both directions.

If the five Pacific countries were to establish PAFTA, they should welcome as associated members those developing countries in Asia and Latin America who wish to join. Or, they might provide PAFTA preferential tariffs in favour of the developing countries. Moreover, the five Pacific countries should provide more effective assistance on a larger scale to foster structural adjustment within their own economies in order to open wider markets for developing-country exports. Concerted policy measures among the five Pacific countries are urgently required for this purpose.

In this context, Japan's attitude towards mainland China might present problems. Political, military and ideological troubles aside, however, it is obvious that the main supply sources for natural resources and the most profitable markets for Japan are not on the Asian mainland but within the extended Pacific region.

Although the establishment of a Pacific Free Trade Area seems quite beneficial to Japan, there is hesitation and/or caution in Japan about stepping out in that direction. One of the reasons for hesitation is. that agriculture remains heavily protected and agricultural rationalisation will take considerable time. The other is fear about the penetration and domination of American capital. These difficulties and worries should be subordinated to a wider view of economic co-operation within the extended Pacific region.

The proposal for the formation of a North Atlantic Free Trade Area[11] deserves attention. The NAFTA proposal aims at the establishment of a broad, open-ended, Atlantic-based free-trade area embracing almost all industrially advanced nations, but its core is to be Britain, Canada and the United States. Proposals for integration between Canada and the United States have a much longer history,[12] but the suggested North American–United Kingdom link is of more recent origin. If only non-agricultural trade is freed among Canada, Britain and the United States, the Maxwell Stamp report estimates that Britain's balance of trade in manufactures with the United States and Canada 'would improve quite substantially in NAFTA provided British export prices could be held down',[13] and the improvement would be far greater than Britain's joining the E.E.C. A larger part of these increases in British exports in NAFTA are brought about from the trade-diversion effect than from the trade-creation effect. The report calculated that 'the U.K. would deflect $261 m. of E.E.C. exports from the U.S. market and $43 m. from the Canadian market. On similar assumptions the U.K. could capture about 10 per cent[14] of Japanese trade in North American markets, if Japan were not in NAFTA' (see Table 7.1).[15]

Table 7.1. Effects on United Kingdom Trade Balance of Joining NAFTA and E.E.C.

(million U.S. dollars)

	NAFTA			E.E.C.
	U.S.	Canada	Total	
Export increase				
Trade creation	243	49	292	316
Trade diversion	485	67	552	191
Import increase	186	3	189	286
Gain to trade balance	542	113	655	221

The NAFTA plan treats Japan, Australia and New Zealand lightly, although it allows for their accommodation as fringe members. From our standpoint, this hardly seems satisfactory. What course, then, should Japan, Australia and New Zealand follow in the Pacific?

If NAFTA were successfully initiated among Britain, Canada and the United States prior to the establishment of closer Pacific integration, Japan should not hesitate to opt for NAFTA membership, else she would suffer large-scale trade-diversion effects.[16] Since the NAFTA proposal only aims at freeing non-agricultural trade, Australia and New Zealand would probably be less interested in joining.[17]

Both for NAFTA and PAFTA, a crucial question is: 'Would the Americans accept the free trade area concept of a new Grand Design?'[18] If so, PAFTA and NAFTA might be linked together through the United States and Canada, which are included in both free-trade area proposals. The United States could move towards the free-trade area approach if multilateral, non-discriminatory approaches to the reduction of tariff and non-tariff barriers prove too difficult within the next five years. It is to be hoped that the new Administration resists following the course of protectionism and isolationism that otherwise might gather strength.[19]

It should be noted that the Pacific-basin countries have their own reasons for promoting economic integration through the establishment of PAFTA and a Pacific Currency Area. Their major interests differ widely from those of Europeans. The Pacific-basin region has a huge potential for trade growth and development which should be cultivated through co-ordinated efforts. Countries belonging to this region have already given recognition to the twin common aims of promoting freer trade growth among five Pacific advanced countries and of expanding aid and trade growth between these advanced countries and neighbouring less developed countries. Regional solidarity in measures for supporting the dollar so that American economic potential can exercise a more positive role is urgently required. Solidarity in the political and military objectives of these countries could also be developed further.

Even if PAFTA would seem likely to be ultimately linked with the NAFTA scheme, prior progress towards trade liberalisation

173

within both the Pacific and Atlantic regions is desirable. A broad free-trade agreement covering a wide range of commitments could be most readily negotiated within a small group. The unification of PAFTA and NAFTA could eventually become possible through some measure similar to the dominant supplier authority of the United States Trade Expansion Act of 1962.

Thus, a Pacific Free Trade Area is by no means isolated with an Atlantic Free Trade Area; rather, the two represent complementary instruments for advancing towards the ultimate objective of freer world trade.

In the event that the United States hesitates to move towards any kind of free-trade area approach, another alternative presents itself: that is, the proposal for a Japanese–Australian–New Zealand free-trade area or Western Pacific economic integration. 'For the nearer term,' Harry G. Johnson pointed out, 'it would seem more realistic to concentrate attention on the probable benefits, drawbacks, and constitutional problems of a narrower Pacific free trade arrangement among Australia, New Zealand, and Japan. . . . A free trade area among these three countries could in addition – like EFTA in the European context – serve as a pilot model of free trade for the rest of the world, and possibly in the course of time be one of the building blocks out of which a world-wide system to free trade could be constructed.'[20]

In 1965 the total population of the three countries was approximately 115 million, which is 35 million less than the population of the European Economic Community immediately prior to its formation. In 1965 Australia's gross national product was $U.S. 21,587 million, Japan's G.N.P. $U.S. 84,324 million and New Zealand's G.N.P. $U.S. 3,933 million, giving a G.N.P. for the entire area in 1965 of approximately $U.S. 110,000 million. On a per capita basis the relevant figures are Australia $U.S. 1,900, Japan $U.S. 861 and New Zealand $U.S. 1,490, which gives an average per capita income for the area as a whole of $U.S. 981. In real terms this figure compares favourably with that of the E.E.C. countries in 1955.[21]

Since the enforcement of the Australia–New Zealand Free Trade Agreement in January 1966, the two countries have endeavoured to promote economic integration, but with some

174

difficulty, because of the lack of fundamental complementarity and because the small size of both economies prevents realisation of economies of scale. It is expected that closer union with a large complementary economy, like Japan, would make Western Pacific integration more successful and fruitful. Thus, the gains from trade liberalisation among the three countries and the feasibility of sectoral integration in such key industries as motor vehicles, iron and steel, non-ferrous metals (especially aluminium) and meat and dairy products have been explored.[22]

The negotiability of a free-trade area among these countries faces two main problems: first, the existing Japanese policies of agricultural protection, and secondly, Australian and New Zealand policies of protection for their manufacturing industries. Moreover, while JANFTA could be of considerable benefit to the Australian and New Zealand economies, the small increase in the size of Japan's market deriving from union diminishes the importance of the benefits.

The formation of a free-trade area or the alternative of closer economic co-operation among Australia, New Zealand and Japan is important from two points of view. First, it would accelerate economic growth, based upon the highly complementary nature of the three economies, and it would strengthen their capacity to export to third countries outside the area, especially to North American and Western European markets. It would also be useful for the three countries to develop a negotiating bloc for obtaining concessions on a broader front, especially from the United States. A free-trade area between these three countries is justifiable and necessary as a means of preparing a favourable position for their joining, or for their providing a jolt towards the formation of, a Pacific Free Trade Area or a wider free-trade area among almost all industrial nations.

Secondly, closer co-operation between Australia, New Zealand and Japan is especially desirable in order to increase aid to and facilitate trade growth with neighbouring Asian developing countries in which the three countries are greatly interested and commonly involved.

Obviously, the establishment of a Pacific Free Trade Area is far from realisation. But publicity for the benefits of free trade in whatever form will be salutary in the post-Kennedy Round

175

era, as the forces of protectionism threaten to gather strength. Exploration of the probable effects of a Pacific Free Trade Area and a Pacific Currency Area will enable the formation of better trade and monetary policies even though they fall short of the desired objective. And study of these proposals in the context of the development problem is independently useful in working towards some solution to the North–South problem, one of the most important problems that has been side-stepped in the process of trade liberalisation in the post-war world.

Notes

1. Japan consists of many small and mountainous islands. The total area is 370,000 sq. km., less than one-twentieth the size of the United States or Australia, with a total population of more than 96 million in 1965 and 103 million in 1970.

2. See Kiyoshi Kojima, 'Capital Accumulation and the Course of Industrialization, with Special Reference to Japan', *Economic Journal* (Dec. 1960), pp. 757–68.

3. Kiyoshi Kojima, 'Economic Development and Import Dependence in Japan', *Hitotsubashi Journal of Economics* (Oct. 1960).

4. These estimates were made for the year 1963 by the Economic Planning Agency. Only direct inputs of imported materials are included in the figures.

5. Calculated from *United Nations Yearbook of National Accounts Statistics and the Growth of World Industry* (New York, 1963).

6. The concept of 'intensities of trade' was first used in A. J. Brown, *Applied Economics: Aspects of the World Economy in War and Peace* (London, 1947), pp. 212–26.

7. In symbols:

$$\frac{X_{ij}}{X_i} \bigg/ \frac{M_j}{W - M_i}$$

where X_{ij} stands for Japanese exports to country j; X_i for total Japanese exports; M_j for total imports by country j; M_i for total imports by Japan; and W for total world trade.

8. In symbols:

$$\frac{X_{ji}}{X_j} \bigg/ \frac{M_i}{W - M_j}$$

where X_{ji} stands for Japanese imports from country j; X_j for total exports by country j; M_i, M_j and W are the same as in the preceding note.

9. Bela Balassa, *Trade Liberalization among Industrial Countries: Objectives and Alternatives* (McGraw-Hill, New York, 1967), pp. 199–227. The indices of relative export and import performance are shown in symbols:

$$\frac{X_{ih}}{X_{nh}} \bigg/ \frac{X_{it}}{X_{nt}} \times 100$$

where X represents exports and the subscript i relates to Japan, n to industrial countries, h a given commodity, and t all commodities.

10. The classification is somewhat arbitrary. After having taken 150 as the benchmark for the strong advantage group, the upper limit of the weak advantage group has been given as the reciprocal of 150, multiplied by 10,000. Only export performance indices have been considered because these appear to be more reliable

177

than indices of export–import ratios which are greatly affected by the level of protection in individual industries.

11. It will be perceived that the number of commodities which moved from a lower to a higher group exceeds the number for which the reverse is true. This may seem strange at first sight, since the weighted average of the export performance indices must necessarily equal 100. But the declining importance of commodities with a large relative share in trade has allowed for an upgrading of a greater number of commodities. These developments give expression to the transformation and diversification of Japan's manufactured exports, which is also reflected in the declining dispersion of export performance: the standard deviation of these indices fell from 127·7 in 1953–5 to 117·7 in 1960–2.

12. On this point see Bela Balassa, 'Tariff Reductions and Trade in Manufactures among the Industrial Countries', *American Economic Review* (June 1966), pp. 466–73.

13. Using the revised S.I.T.C. classification, the following products come into the four groups:

A group: Sections 0, 1, 2 (excluding 251, 266, 267, 27 and 28), 4 and subgroup 941.0.

N group: Divisions 27, 28 and Section 3.

L group: Sections 6 (excluding 67, 68 and 661–4) and 8, and groups 267, 541 and 733.

K group: Sections 5 (excluding 541) and 7 (excluding 733), divisions 67 and 68, and groups 251, 266 and 661–4.

14. It should be added that the ratio of 83 for 1960–2 was due to a large extent to the high transport costs of primary goods which account for three-fourths of Japan's imports. Transportation costs are included in the c.i.f. price of imports, while exports are valued at f.o.b. prices. The ratio approaches 100 if both exports and imports are valued on an f.o.b. basis.

15. Still, the degree of horizontal trade in K goods is smaller in the case of Japan than for any of the other industrial countries, and Japan has practically no horizontal trade in light manufactures, though such trade is substantial for other industrial countries. See Kiyoshi Kojima, 'The Pattern of International Trade among Advanced Countries', *Hitotsubashi Journal of Economics*, v 1 (June 1964), 16–36.

16. In symbols:

$$\frac{X_{ij}^h}{X_{ij}} \Big/ \frac{M_j^h}{M}$$

where X_{ij}^h is Japan's exports of commodity h to country j; X_{ij} is Japan's total exports to country j; M_j^h country j's imports of commodity h from all sources of supply; and M_j country j's total imports.

17. In symbols:

$$\frac{X_{ij}^h}{X_{ij}} \Big/ \frac{X_i^h}{X_i}$$

where X_{ij}^h and X_{ij} are as explained in note 16 above; X_i^h stands for Japan's exports of commodity h to the whole world; and X_i is Japan's total exports.

18. Cf. Japanese Ministry of International Trade and Industry, *Annual Report on Foreign Trade* (Tokyo, 1961).

19. Japan's exports appear to increase by 1·3039 for every unit increase in her imports from Asian sterling area countries, the corresponding figures being 1·4149

178

for other Asian countries, as against 0·7945 for the United States and 0·9650 for the European Economic Community. These 'reflection ratios', calculated by the Japanese Economic Planning Agency, show the sum of direct effects of a unit change in imports, and are based upon an international trade matrix for an average of 1960 and 1961.

20. Economic Planning Agency, *Japan's Economic Survey for 1962*, pp. 435–6.

21. Professor Balassa has suggested that export prices in Western Europe might be assumed to increase by one-half of the absolute tariff reduction. While this assumption is not made here, the results are hardly affected thereby since Japan's trade with European countries is rather small.

22. B. J. Ball and K. Marwah, 'The U.S. Demand for Imports, 1948–1958', *Review of Economics and Statistics* (Nov. 1962), pp. 355–401.

23. This ratio indicates the percentage of liberalised items in the total value of imports in 1959, excluding governmental imports.

24. The time period covered for each commodity group varies, since the imports were liberalised at varying intervals.

25. Quantitative import restriction of automobiles was abolished, in fact, in September 1965.

Chapter 2

1. Roy Harrod, 'Economic Development and Asian Regional Co-operation' *Pakistan Development Review*, II 1 (spring 1962), 16.

2. Ibid., p. 14. So far as I am aware, Gunnar Myrdal was the first to express a similar idea. He argued the need for 'second-grade international specialisation' among less developed countries. 'It would require co-operative planning and not only co-operative discrimination. On the basis of such planning, one country would allow preferential terms for imports of a particular product from another country in exchange for similar treatment on the part of that country in regard to another product; and this agreement would then have to be followed up by a planned increase of the investments for production of the two products in the respective countries.' Gunnar Myrdal, *An International Economy: Problems and Prospects* (Harper & Bros, New York, 1956), pp. 259, 261. In a paper entitled 'The Efforts toward Integration in Rich and Poor Countries', delivered in Mexico City on 3 Oct., 1966, he suggested that a common market among less developed countries 'must be completed by formal agreements, reached after negotiation, concerning what industries should be located in what countries. When thought through with all its consequences, this implies the need for a joint common planning.' Quoted by Hal B. Lary, *Imports of Manufactures from Less Developed Countries* (National Bureau of Economic Research, New York, 1968), p. 12 fn.

3. Excellent surveys of the underlying causes of these changes in international specialisation are provided by J. Bhagwati, 'The Pure Theory of International Trade', *Economic Journal* (Mar. 1964), pp. 1–84; and Harry G. Johnson, *Comparative Cost and Commercial Policy Theory for a Developing World Economy*, the Wicksell Lecture for 1968 (Stockholm, 1968).

4. Broadly speaking, developments in the theory of international trade from Ricardo to recent theory which emphasises the R. & D. factor in trade specialisation, can be seen in terms of explicit stress on a couple of dominant factors of production (or perhaps only one factor). The stress depends on the type of countries and the stages in their development which are being analysed. This way of thinking

is seen typically in S. Hirsch, *Location of Industry and International Competitiveness* (Oxford, 1967), appendix to chap. ii, pp. 34–41.

5. See Ragnar Nurkse, *Patterns of Trade and Development*, Wicksell Lectures, 1959 (Stockholm, 1959), pp. 13–19, for an excellent analysis of these developments. See also GATT, *International Trade, 1959–1960* (Geneva, 1960), pt. i; and United Nations, *World Economic Survey, 1958* (New York, 1959), pt. i, chap. 1.

6. Lary, op. cit., p. 48.

7. As described by Gunnar Myrdal in *Economic Theory and Underdeveloped Regions* (Duckworth, London, 1957), pp. 27–33.

8. For an ingenious formal presentation of the theory of immiserising growth, see J. Bhagwati, 'Immiserizing Growth: A Geometrical Note', *Review of Economic Studies* (June 1958) and 'International Trade and Economic Expansion', *American Economic Review* (Dec. 1958).

9. Jacob Viner, *The Customs Union Issue* (Carnegie Endowment for International Peace, New York, 1950), p. 43.

10. R. G. Lipsey, 'The Theory of Customs Union: A General Survey', *Economic Journal* (Sep. 1956), p. 499. Lipsey's article provides an excellent review of the main issues. My own thoughts about the issue of integration were originally published in *Hitotsubashi Ronso* (Sep. 1962), in Japanese. Recent contributions by C. A. Cooper and B. F. Massell, and Harry G. Johnson, lead to conclusions similar to those in my Japanese paper.

11. Ibid., p. 501.

12. C. A. Cooper and B. F. Massell, 'A New Look at Customs Union Theory', *Economic Journal* (Dec. 1965), p. 745.

13. Harry G. Johnson, 'An Economic Theory of Protectionism, Tariff Bargaining, and the Formation of Customs Union', *Journal of Political Economy* (June 1965), pp. 256–83.

14. Ibid., p. 270.

15. J. F. Deniau, *The Common Market, Its Structure and Purpose* (London, 1960), p. 16.

16. Ibid., p. 15.

17. Tibor Scitovsky, *Economic Theory and Western European Integration* (Allen & Unwin, London, 1958), p. 31; see also Don D. Humphrey, 'The Effects of a Customs Union in Western Europe', *Southern Economic Journal* (Apr. 1961), pp. 283–4.

18. Scitovsky, op. cit., p. 31.

19. Walter Isard, *Location and the Space Economy* (New York, 1956), chap. viii. Balassa refers to location theory as one of the important ingredients of the theory of economic integration. Bela Balassa, 'Towards a Theory of Economic Integration', *Kyklos*, xiv fasc. 1 (1961), 6–8.

20. See E. A. G. Robinson (ed.), *Economic Consequences of the Size of Nations* (Macmillan, London, 1960), p. xviii, who concludes that 'most of the major industrial economies of scale could be achieved by a relatively high-income nation of 50 million; that nations of 10–15 million were probably too small to get all the technical economies available; that the industrial economies of scale beyond a size of 50 million were mainly those that derive from a change in the character of competition and of specialisation.' See also Harry G. Johnson, 'The Criteria of Economic Advantage', in G. D. N. Worswick (ed.), *The Free Trade Proposals* (Oxford, 1960), p. 33.

21. Scitovsky, op. cit., pp. 41, 48.

22. Interestingly, Bertil Ohlin, *Interregional and International Trade*, rev. ed. (Harvard University Press, Cambridge, Mass., 1967), pp. 38–41, recognised increasing returns to scale as a potent cause of trade specialisation. See also Harry G. Johnson, 'International Trade Theory and Monopolistic Competition Theory',

180

in R. E. Kuenne (ed.), *Monopolistic Competition Theory* (Wiley, New York, 1967), p. 205, fn. 9.

23. This kind of envelope curve was developed by Sir Roy Harrod in 'Notes on Supply', *Economic Journal*, XL (1930), 232–41, and 'The Law of Decreasing Costs', *Economic Journal*, XLI (1931), 566–76. See also Jacob Viner, 'Cost Curves and Supply Curves', *Zeitschrift für Nationalökonomie*, III (1931–2), 23–46, reprinted in George J. Stigler and Kenneth E. Boulding (eds), *Readings in Price Theory* (Chicago, 1952), pp. 198–232.

24. For an excellent survey of this subject and areas worth further investigation, see Harry G. Johnson, loc. cit.

25. R. C. O. Matthews, 'Reciprocal Demand and Increasing Returns', *Review of Economic Studies*, XVII (1949–50), 152.

26. J. E. Meade, *A Geometry of International Trade* (Allen & Unwin, London, 1952), p. 33.

27. Matthews, op. cit., p. 152.

28. 'The traditional comparative cost analysis thus is not a reliable predictor of the pattern of national specialisation under conditions of decreasing cost.' Herbert G. Grubel, 'Intra-Industry Specialisation and the Pattern of Trade', *Canadian Journal of Economics and Political Science*, XXXIII (1967), 385.

29. Some alternative paths towards specialisation through the realisation of economies of scale have been suggested. First, Ohlin suggests that increasing returns to scale will be a powerful cause of trade specialisation, arguing that when 'a number of regions are isolated from each other, and . . . their factor endowments and their demand are so balanced that the relative prices of factors and commodities are everywhere the same, . . . no trade is then possible. As a matter of fact, insofar as the market for some articles within each region is not large enough to permit the most efficient scale of production, division of labor and trade will be profitable. Each region will specialize on some of these articles and exchange them for the rest. The character of this trade will be entirely *a matter of chance* if factor equipment is everywhere the same, for it doesn't matter whether a certain region specializes in one commodity or another.' (My italics.) Op. cit., p. 38. Second, Meade concludes that 'in the case of important increasing returns to scale in both countries *a structural jolt* might be able to shift the world economy from one position of stable equilibrium (in which one country specialized wholly on one line of product) to a second position of stable equilibrium (in which that country specialized wholly on the other line of product), and that such a change might be better for both countries, worse for both, or better for one and worse for the other.' (My italics.) Op. cit., pp. 42–3. Finally, L. H. Janssen, in a model similar to mine, stresses that '*Where, however, for political reasons, both countries specialize in the same product, considerable wastage results. Mutual agreements, or perhaps even a supranational form of control, will then be necessary to obtain an optimum result.*' (Author's italics.) *Free Trade, Protection and Customs Union* (H. E. Stenfert Kross N.V., Leiden, 1961), p. 29.

30. The homothetic indifference curves would then be symmetric to a line from A or B less steep than the diagonal of the transformation box. The tangencies of the two indifference maps would yield terms of trade more favourable to x, or steeper than the diagonal MN.

31. Graham justified protection on grounds similar to these. Frank D. Graham, 'Some Aspects of Protection Further Considered', *Quarterly Journal of Economics* (Feb. 1923), pp. 199–227.

32. Johnson, in *J.P.E.* (June 1965), pp. 256–83.

33. See Sidney Dell, *A Latin American Common Market* (Oxford University Press, London, 1966); Miguel S. Wionczek (ed.), *Latin American Economic Integration* (Praeger, New York, 1966).

34. ECAFE, 'Projections of Foreign Trade of the ECAFE Region up to 1980', *Economic Bulletin for Asia and the Far East*, XIV 3 (Dec. 1963), 95. Cf. Bela Balassa, *Economic Development and Integration* (Centro de Estudios Monetarios Latino-americanos, Mexico, 1965), chap. 3; Peter J. Lloyd, *International Trade Problems of Small Nations* (Duke University Press, Durham, N.C., 1968), chap. 7.

35. Raul Prebisch, *Towards a New Trade Policy for Development* (United Nations, New York, 1964) and *Towards a Global Strategy of Development* (United Nations, New York, 1968).

36. Harry G. Johnson, 'Notes on Some Theoretical Problems Posed by the Foreign Trade of Centrally Planned Economies', in Alan A. Brown and Egon Neuberger (eds), *International Trade and Central Planning* (University of California Press, Berkeley and Los Angeles, 1968), p. 395.

37. Gyule Kavásznai and Ferenc Kozma, 'Some Problems of Inter-Industry Co-operation between the Countries of the Council for Mutual Economic Assistance', in Hungarian Academy of Sciences Institute of Economics, *Studies in International Economics* (Akadémiai Kaidó, Budapest, 1966), p. 144.

38. See, for example, Stanislaw Góra and Mieczyslaw Hokowski, 'The Criteria of Intra-Branch Specialization among Socialist Countries', in *Problems of Economic Theory and Practice in Poland*, vol. 2 (Polish Scientific Publishers, Warsaw, 1966); V. P. Sergeyev, 'Economic Principles of the Foreign Trade of Socialist States', in Roy Harrod and D. C. Hague (eds), *International Trade Theory in a Developing World* (Macmillan, London, 1963), pp. 277–96.

39. See D. L. McLachlan and D. Swann, *Competitive Policy in the European Community* (Oxford University Press, London, 1967), chaps 5 (esp. pp. 72–3) and 8.

40. The reorganisation of market and industrial structures in Canada is one of the reasons why a United States–Canada free-trade area has been advocated. S. Stykolt and H. C. Eastman, 'A Model for the Study of Protected Oligopolies', *Economic Journal* (June 1960), pp. 336–47; H. C. Eastman, 'The Canadian Tariff and the Efficiency of the Canadian Economy', *American Economic Review*, LIV (1964), 437–48; H. E. English, *Industrial Structure in Canada's International Competitive Position* (Private Planning Association of Canada, Montreal, 1964); R. J. and P. Wonnacott, *Free Trade between the United States and Canada* (Harvard University Press, Cambridge, Mass., 1967); Canadian–American Committee, *A Canada–U.S. Free Trade Arrangement, Survey of Possible Characteristics* (National Planning Association, Washington, D.C., Oct. 1963); idem., *A Possible Plan for Canada–U.S. Free Trade Area, A Staff Report* (Feb. 1965).

41. Grubel, loc. cit., pp. 375–88; Bela Balassa, 'Tariff Reductions and Trade in Manufactures among the Industrial Countries', *American Economic Review* (June 1966), pp. 466–73.

42. The European Coal and Steel Community provides a representative case. The Canada–United States Automotive Agreement is another successful example. The differentiation of motor-vehicle types produced in various countries has also been planned by multinational enterprises. The development of complementarity industries in LAFTA countries has so far been undertaken mainly by giant American companies. See also Sperry Lea, 'Free Trade by Sectors', in National Planning Association, *Looking Ahead* (Sep. 1966).

Chapter 3

1. If the United Kingdom's reaction to the establishment of PAFTA were favourable, her entry into it would be welcome.

2. Similar associate membership may also be advantageous for Latin American countries.

3. See Chapter 1 for a definition of these concepts.

4. According to the revised S.I.T.C., the coverage of commodity groups is as follows:

N_1 goods: Division 04.

N_2 goods: Sections 0 (less 04) and 1, and 941.

N_3 goods: Sections 2 (less 251, 266, 267, 27, 28) and 4.

N_4 goods: Divisions 27 and 28, and Section 3 (less 351).

L_1 goods: Sections 6 (less 66, 67, 68, 69) and 8 (less 812, 821, 86), and 267, 665, 666, 667.

L_2 goods: 541, 69, 733, 812, 821, 86, 951, 961.

K_1 goods: Section 5 (less 541) and 251, 166, 351, 66 (less 665, 666, 667), 67, 68.

K_2 goods: Section 7 (less 733).

5. Kiyoshi Kojima, 'The Pattern of International Trade among Advanced Countries', *Hitotsubashi Journal of Economics*, v 1 (June 1964), 24–6.

6. The degree of horizontal trade between two countries for a certain commodity category (denoted by D) is calculated as follows: where country A's imports of commodity h from country B is A_h and country B's imports of the same commodity h from country A is B_h:

$$D = \frac{B_h}{A_h} \times 100, \quad \text{if} \quad A_h > B_h \quad \text{or} \quad D = \frac{A_h}{B_h} \times 100, \quad \text{if} \quad A_h < B_h.$$

The degree of aggregate horizontal trade (denoted by $\bar{D}$) can also be calculated as the weighted average of D of several commodities by using as weights the percentage ratio of the total of A_h and B_h in the total trade of the two countries, or it is shown as follows:

$$\bar{D} = \sum \frac{B_h}{A_h} \cdot \frac{A_h + B_h}{M_A + M_B} \quad (\text{if} \quad A_h > B_h)$$

$$+ \sum \frac{A_h}{B_h} \cdot \frac{A_h + B_h}{M_A + M_B} \quad (\text{if} \quad A_h < B_h),$$

where M_A represents country A's total imports from country B, and M_B country B's total imports from country A.

The degree of horizontal trade is always less than 100, and the closer it is to 100, the further the horizontal trade is carried out and balanced within the same commodity category or aggregate categories.

7. It was estimated that the increase would be $U.S. 3,183 million or 23 per cent of the total intra-areal trade in 1963 (Kiyoshi Kojima, 'A Pacific Economic Community and Asian Developing Countries', *Hitotsubashi Journal of Economics*, VII 1 (June 1966), 23–4). The greater increase in 1965 than in 1963 is due to a faster growth in manufactured products trade than in trade of primary products during that period.

Somewhat different, but largely similar, estimates are presented in Bruce W. Wilkinson, 'A Re-estimation of the Effects of the Formation of a Pacific Area Free Trade Agreement', in Kiyoshi Kojima (ed.), *Pacific Trade and Development II* (Japan Economic Research Center, Apr. 1969), pp. 53–95. See also Bruce W. Wilkinson, 'Canadian Trade, the Kennedy Round and a Pacific Free Trade Area', in Kiyoshi Kojima (ed.), *Pacific Trade and Development* (Japan Economic Research Center, Feb. 1968), p. 53; and Peter Drysdale, 'Pacific Economic Integration: An Australian View', ibid., p. 207.

8. Trade diversion effects are not estimated here. If these are included, the expansion of PAFTA trade would be much larger than our estimates show.

9. The rate of increase in a country's exports is proportional to (a) the rate of tariff reductions and (b) the coverage of area which reduces tariffs for the country's exports. Let r_F and r_G stand for the rate of tariff reductions in the case of free-trade area and of global negotiation respectively, and x_F and x_G for the share in a country's total exports to the free-trade area and to the countries which reduce tariffs outside the free-trade area in global negotiation respectively. Then, as $x_F/(x_F + x_G)$ is greater than, equal to or smaller than r_G/r_F, the increase of a country's exports in the case of free-trade area is greater than, equal to or smaller than that in the case of global tariff reductions. For the five Pacific countries taken together, in 1965, $x_F = 0.37$, $x_G = 0.28$ and $x_F/(x_F + x_G) = 0.57$. This is greater than $r_G/r_F = 0.3/1$, and therefore, the establishment of PAFTA would bring about greater trade gains than global tariff reductions on the scale of the Kennedy Round.

10. GATT, *International Trade, 1963* (Geneva, 1964), pp. 10–17.

11. ECAFE, 'Projections of Foreign Trade of the ECAFE Region up to 1980', *Economic Bulletin for Asia and the Far East*, XIV 3 (Dec. 1963).

Chapter 4

1. These estimates were originally published in Japanese in *Kanzei Chosa Geppo* (Ministry of Finance), XX 3 (Apr.–May 1967), and summarised in the *Economist* (Tokyo), 29 Aug. 1967.

2. If β is 1, then $\beta \cdot (t/1 + t)$ simply becomes $(t/1 + t)$ in equations (1) and (2).

3. If the initial P is taken to be 1, M represents both the volume and value of imports.

4. The price elasticity of demand for Japan's imports, η_j, is calculated by use of the formula:

$$\eta_j = \theta \left(\frac{P}{M} \epsilon_d + \frac{C}{M} \eta_d \right)$$

where θ is the elasticity of domestic prices in response to changes in the prices of competitive imports; P/M is the ratio of domestic production to competitive imports from developing countries; C/M is the ratio of consumption to imports; ϵ_d is the price elasticity of domestic supply; and η_d is the price elasticity of domestic demand. It is assumed that θ equals 0.5 for all commodity categories; P/M is 4 for all commodity categories; C/M therefore equals 5 for all commodity categories (i.e. $C = P + M$); ϵ_d equals 0.1 for semi-processed intermediate manufactures, 0.2 for highly processed intermediate manufactures, and 0.4 for finished manufactures; and η_d equals 0.2, 0.3 and 0.5 for the same commodity categories respectively. Hence, η_j is 0.7 for semi-processed intermediate manufactures, 1.2 for highly processed intermediate manufactures, and 2.1 for finished manufactures. These values for η_j are not unrealistic, and they conform well with Tatemoto's estimated elasticity of 1.57 for all imported commodities, over 80 per cent of which are low-elasticity primary commodities (Motohiro Tatemoto, *Econometric Analysis of Foreign Trade* [in Japanese] (Tokyo, 1963), chap. 2).

Similar methods for assuming elasticities of import demand are used, for example, by Bela Balassa, 'Tariff Protection in Industrial Countries: An Evaluation', *Journal of Political Economy* (Dec. 1965), p. 592, and by John E. Floyd, 'The

184

Overvaluation of the Dollar: A Note on the International Price Mechanism', *American Economic Review* (Mar. 1965), pp. 95–107.

Practically no estimates are available for the price elasticity of export supply, ϵ. It is calculated according to the formula:

$$\epsilon = \left(\frac{C}{X}\right)\eta_d + \left(\frac{P}{X}\right)\epsilon_d$$

where C/X stands for the ratio of domestic consumption to exports in each commodity category, and P/X stands for the ratio of domestic production to exports. Using Japanese data for commodity groups isolated here, C/X is assumed to be 2, and P/X is assumed to be 3 for all commodity categories, whilst the values used for η_d and ϵ_d are those used above. Thus, ϵ is 0·7 for semi-processed intermediate manufactures, 1·2 for highly processed intermediate manufactures, and 2·2 for finished manufactures. These values are those commonly used for developing countries (ϵ_u) and Japan (ϵ_j).

5. On average, π_x, the percentage increase in the price of developing-country exports, would be about 8·6 per cent.

6. The method used for assuming elasticities is the same as that explained in note 4 above. The price elasticity of American import demand, η, is assumed to be 0·9 for semi-processed intermediate manufactures, 1·4 for highly processed intermediate manufactures, and 2·5 for finished manufactures. These values are higher than those used for Japan, since C/M (= 5·0) and P/M (= 6·0) are assumed to be larger for the United States. The above values for η may be compared with those derived in the Ball–Marwah study, for example, which are 0·26 for crude materials, 1·38 for semi-manufactures, and 3·5 for finished manufactures (B. J. Ball and K. Marwah, 'The U.S. Demand for Imports, 1948–1958', *Review of Economics and Statistics* (Nov. 1962), pp. 395–401). Imports from developing countries and Japan, which are the subject of this study, consist largely of labour-intensive and less sophisticated manufactures with lower elasticities, so that the lower elasticities assumed for finished manufactures are not inconsistent with the Ball–Marwah figures.

7. Mamoru Okita, 'Impacts on Japanese Trade of Preferences to Developing Countries', *Economist* (Tokyo), 26 Sep., 1967 (in Japanese).

8. Bureau of Customs, Ministry of Finance, *A Report on Preferences*, 11 Oct. 1967.

9. Harry G. Johnson, 'Trade Preferences and Developing Countries', *Lloyds Bank Review* (Apr. 1966), p. 18; Harry G. Johnson, *Economic Policies toward Less Developed Countries* (Brookings Institution, Washington, D.C., 1967), chap. 6.

10. See Gardner Patterson, *Discrimination in International Trade: The Policy Issues, 1945–1965* (Princeton, 1966), pp. 358–9, 381–3; John Pincus, *Trade, Aid and Development* (Council on Foreign Relations, 1967), chap. 6. Pincus, p. 231, estimates that a general preference scheme could increase the export receipts of developing countries by the general order of $U.S. 1 billion annually if processed products were included. This estimate is the largest of several estimates made.

11. Grant L. Reuber, *Canada's Interest in the Trade Problems of Less-Developed Countries* (Canadian Trade Committee and Private Planning Association of Canada, 1964), p. xii.

12. See Johnson, in *Lloyds Bank Review* (Apr. 1966), pp. 13–17, and Bela Balassa, 'The Structure of Protection in the Industrial Countries and its Effects on the Exports of Processed Goods from Developing Countries', *I.B.R.D. Report*, no. EC-152a (Feb. 1968).

13. Prebisch, *Towards a New Trade Policy for Development*.

14. See David Wall, *The Third World Challenge: Preferences for Development* (Atlantic Trade Study, London, 1967), pp. 44–8.

15. See Donald McDougall and Rosemary Hutt, 'Imperial Preference: A Quantitative Analysis', *Economic Journal* (June 1954), p. 269.

Chapter 5

1. UNCTAD, *The Significance of the Second Session of UNCTAD*, Report to the Secretary-General of the United Nations, TD/96, 7 May 1968.

2. See, for example, David Howell, 'Failure at UNCTAD II', *The Round Table* (July 1968), pp. 249–53.

3. Lary, *Imports of Manufactures from Less Developed Countries*, p. 19. Total value added per employee, which is taken to represent the difference in capital intensity in thirteen industry groups, is compared among nine countries (the United States, Canada, Australia, Sweden, the United Kingdom, Japan, Brazil, Mexico and India), and both Kendall's coefficient of concordance (0·853) and chi-square test (92·12) are very significant (ibid., p. 71).

4. Kiyoshi Kojima, 'Structure of Comparative Advantage in Industrial Countries: A Verification of the Factor-Proportions Theorem', *Hitotsubashi Journal of Economics* (June 1970).

5. Lary, op. cit., Preface, p. xv.

6. Johnson, *Economic Policies toward Less Developed Countries*, pp. 201–4.

7. David Wall, *The Third World Challenge: Preferences for Development*, pp. 61–2.

8. See Wall, ibid., and 'Markets for the Underdeveloped', *The Round Table* (Oct. 1968), pp. 406–7.

9. A more detailed explanation is presented in Kiyoshi Kojima, 'A Proposal for International Aid', in *The Developing Economies* (Institute of Asian Economic Affairs, Tokyo, Dec. 1964), pp. 337–57.

10. Saburo Okita and Akira Ohnishi, 'Japan's Role in Asian Economic Development', in Kojima (ed.), *Pacific Trade and Development*, pp. 360–1.

11. Some estimates were attempted in Chapter 3 above.

12. David Wall, *The Third World Challenge: Preferences for Development*, p. 65.

13. The UNCTAD scheme of general preferences creates new discrimination, while F.T.A. preference would prevent increased discrimination.

Chapter 6

1. The best explanation of the S.D.R. system is, so far as I am aware, in Fritz Machlup, *The Rio Agreement and Beyond: Remaking the International Monetary System*, C.E.D. Supplementary Paper No. 24 (Johns Hopkins Press, Baltimore, 1968).

2. Warning of this was given by Robert Triffin, in *Gold and the Dollar Crisis: The Future of Convertibility* (Yale University Press, 1960).

3. Ibid.

4. If S.D.R.s are created to the extent of $U.S. 3 billion annually, they will amount to $U.S. 15 billion in five years. This can be compared with about $U.S. 40 billion worth of monetary gold in the world or $U.S. 12·1 billion worth in the United States.

5. Milton Friedman, 'The Case for Flexible Exchange Rates', in his *Essays in Positive Economics* (Chicago, 1953); Egon Sohmen, *Flexible Exchange Rates* (Chicago,

1961). See also Milton Friedman and Robert V. Roosa, *The Balance of Payments: Free versus Fixed Exchange Rates* (Washington, D.C., 1967).

6. G. N. Halm, *The 'Band' Proposal: The Limits of Permissible Exchange Rate Variations*, Special Studies in International Economics, No. 6 (Princeton University, Jan. 1965).

7. J. E. Meade, 'The International Monetary Mechanism', *Three Banks Review* (Sep. 1964); J. H. Williamson, *The Crawling Peg*, Essays in International Finance, No. 50 (Princeton University, Dec. 1965).

8. Gold revaluation was advocated by Roy F. Harrod, 'Imbalance of International Payments', *I.M.F. Staff Papers* (Apr. 1953) and explained by Jacques Rueff, 'The Rueff Approach', in Randall Hinshaw (ed.), *Monetary Reform and the Price of Gold: Alternative Approaches* (Johns Hopkins Press, Baltimore, 1967).

9. This problem was explored by Zentaro Matsumura, 'An Evolutionary Plan for World Monetary Reform', *The Banker* (Sep. 1966).

10. See especially Chapter 3.

11. Robert A. Mundell, *The International Monetary System: Conflict and Reform* (Private Planning Association of Canada, July 1965), p. 6.

12. Harry G. Johnson, 'A New World Trade Policy in the Post-Kennedy Round Era: A Survey of Alternatives, with Special Reference to the Position of the Pacific and Asian Regions', in Kojima (ed.), *Pacific Trade and Development*, pp. 246–7.

13. Ronald I. McKinnon recommends the formation of an optimum currency area for the E.E.C. or Western Europe in his 'Optimum World Money Arrangements and the Dual Currency System', *Banca Nazionale del Lavoro Quarterly Review*, XVI (1963).

14. It is worth noting that Japan's foreign exchange reserves have increased rapidly since 1968.

15. Richard N. Cooper, 'Financial Aspects of Economic Cooperation around the Pacific', in Kojima (ed.), *Pacific Trade and Development*.

16. Algebraically, the standard deviation (σ_n) of combined reserve changes for n countries is given by the expression:

$$\sigma_n = \sqrt{\sum_i \sigma_i^2 + 2\sum_i \sum_{j>i} r_{ij}\, \sigma_i\, \sigma_j}\,.$$

The expression in root will be smaller, the smaller are the correlation coefficients $r_{ij}(i, j = 1, 2, \ldots, n)$. σ_n will equal the sum of the individual standard deviation σ_i only if $r_{ij} = 1$ for all i, j.

17. This amounts to 44 per cent for the period 1955–66 according to Cooper, loc. cit., p. 299.

18. Ibid.

19. Mundell, op. cit., pp. 39–43, 61–2.

20. Cf. Joan Robinson, 'The Foreign Exchange', in her *Essays in the Theory of Employment* (London, 1947). The simplest stability condition is that the sum of price elasticities of import demands in home and foreign countries should be greater than unity. See A. P. Lerner, *The Economics of Control* (New York, 1964), p. 378.

21. The way in which the price elasticity of export supplies would change with the formation of an optimum currency area may be analysed in a similar fashion. The analysis of export elasticities has not been undertaken here since the most important element in the effectiveness of exchange changes is the elasticity of import demand, rather than export supply.

22. Cf. Robert A. Mundell, 'Theory of Optimum Currency Areas', *American Economic Review* (Sep. 1961), p. 663.

23. James E. Meade, 'The Case for Variable Exchange Rates', *Three Banks Review* (Sep. 1955) and 'The Future of International Trade and Payments', *Three Banks Review* (June 1961).

24. Mundell, in *AER* (Sep. 1961), p. 664; McKinnon, loc. cit., pp. 372–3.

25. A third view has been put by Johnson, who argued that 'it might be preferable for members to move to exchange rates fluctuating freely in relation to the currencies of the other members as well as the currencies of nonmembers'. Harry G. Johnson, 'The Monetary Implication of a Free Trade Association', in Thomas M. Franck and Edward Weisband (eds.), *A Free Trade Association* (New York University Press, 1968), p. 239.

26. Cooper, loc. cit., p. 287.

27. Ibid., p. 287.

28. Balassa, *Trade Liberalization among Industrial Countries*, pp. 160–1.

29. A.I.D. aid was 41 per cent 'tied aid' in 1960, but this proportion rose to 95 per cent by 1967. See *A.I.D. Quarterly Report*, 'Trend of A.I.D. Commodity Expenditures of Procurement by Resources' (Washington, 1968).

30. See, for example, Mahbub ul Haq, 'Tied Credits: A Quantitative Analysis', in J. H. Adler (ed.), *Capital Movements* (Macmillan, New York, 1967), pp. 326–59.

31. Kiyoshi Kojima, 'A Proposal for Increasing International Liquidity', *Oriental Economist* (Aug. 1964). The proposal was reviewed by the *Economist* (London), 25 July 1964, pp. 401–2, under the headline of 'How Aid Could be Untied'. It was also recorded in *International Monetary Arrangements: The Problem of Choice* (International Finance Section, Princeton University, 1964), p. 88, as follows: '*Deposits of Portions of Aid or Loans Received.* An alternative way of ensuring that aid and loan funds do not cause strain on the donors' payments balance is for a small fixed portion of such funds to be deposited by the recipients in special loan accounts at the I.M.F.; and for those to be drawn on for all expenditures out of such loans to third countries. Countries receiving such deposits in payments for goods and services would be able to transfer these loan deposits for their own settlement, but could not convert them into gold. These "loan deposits" would be liquidated when the loans in question were repaid.'

32. An excellent proposal of an Asian (or ECAFE) Reserve System was presented by Robert Triffin, *Payments Arrangements within ECAFE Region*, Paper No. 114 (Economic Growth Center, Yale University, 1967) and 'International Monetary Cooperation in Asia and the Far East', in Kojima (ed.), *Pacific Trade and Development II*. Since the study was sponsored by the ECAFE, the Reserve System was designed for Asian developing countries and Japan, Australia and New Zealand. It might be wiser, as in our scheme, to establish P.C.A. between five Pacific advanced countries and invite Asian–Latin American participation.

33. In connection with the North Atlantic Free Trade Area, Sir Roy Harrod stressed a similar view, saying that 'It has been noted earlier that it might be expected that the NAFTA group would be like-minded in thinking that aid to the less developed countries should be increased. It might be possible to tie aid, not to the donor country, but to the NAFTA group as a whole. Thus grants provided by one NAFTA country would be usable in any of the NAFTA countries. . . . To the extent that the donor was injured by his funds being spent in another NAFTA country instead of in his own, this damage should be, in part at least, offset by the arrangement for reshuffling gold outlined above.' Sir Roy Harrod, *Dollar–Sterling Collaboration: Basis for Initiative* (Atlantic Trade Study, London, 1967), p. 67. The arrangement for reshuffling gold means that 'The NAFTA countries could agree that each one of their own gold holdings should rise or fall in the same proportion, quite irrespective of their individual balance of payments. This could be achieved by a swapping of gold against currencies within the group.' Ibid., pp. 65–6. The

reserve pooling in our Pacific Currency Area scheme may satisfy more completely this kind of condition.

34. 'The best alternative to a system of fixed rates with provision for increasing liquidity, in our view, would be a modified system of flexible exchange rates consisting of a dollar–sterling bloc and an E.E.C. bloc. There would be relatively fixed rates within each bloc and flexible rates between them. Adoption of this system would imply cutting the tie between gold and the dollar.' Walter Salant and associates, *The United States Balance of Payments in 1968* (Brookings Institution, Washington, D.C., 1963), p. 259.

35. The Asian Development Bank could perform the function of a Lent Currency Scheme if its membership were extended appropriately to embrace those countries designed by the scheme. In that case, the task of a Pacific Bank would be confined to the pooling of reserves and other measures which are necessary for a Pacific Currency Area. However, since it would not be easy for the Asian Development Bank to embrace Latin American countries, only a part of the function of a Lent Currency Scheme could be entrusted to the A.D.B.

36. The Brookings Report supposes, as in note 34 above, a dollar–sterling bloc and an E.E.C. bloc. McKinnon argues for a dual currency world between Western Europe (with the possible exception of Britain) and North America. McKinnon, loc. cit., pp. 379–85. Mundell expects three blocs to emerge, saying that 'the result might be a monetary division of the free world into the *sterling area* (much of the old British Commonwealth, Scandinavia, and the Middle East), the *thaler area* (composed of Continental Europe and some of Africa), and the *dollar area* (the United States, Japan, Canada, most of Latin America, and parts of the rest of the world).' Mundell, *The International Monetary System: Conflict and Reform*, pp. 47–8.

37. Robert Triffin, *Our International Monetary System: Yesterday, Today, and Future* (Random House, New York, 1968), p. 153.

Chapter 7

1. Maxwell Stamp Associates, *The Free Trade Area Option: Opportunity for Britain* (Atlantic Trade Study, London, 1967). See also Theodore Geiger and Sperry Lea, 'The Free Trade Area Concept as Applied to the United States', in *Issues and Objectives of U.S. Foreign Trade Policy: A Compendium of Statements* (Congress of the United States, Sep. 1967).

2. See, for example, Sperry Lea, 'The Future Shape of U.S. Trade Policy: Multilateral or Free Trade Approaches?', in Kojima (ed.), *Pacific Trade and Development II*.

3. A comment against PAFTA is presented by H. W. Arndt, 'PAFTA: An Australian Assessment', *Intereconomics* (Hamburg, Oct. 1967), (reprinted in his *A Small Rich Industrial Country: Studies in Australian Development, Aid and Trade* (Melbourne, 1968)), to which there is a reply by Kiyoshi Kojima, 'A Pacific Free Trade Area Reconsidered', ibid. (Mar. 1968). There also exists a favourable Australian view of PAFTA, for example Peter Drysdale, 'Pacific Economic Integration: An Australian View', in Kojima (ed.), *Pacific Trade and Development*.

4. Johnson, in Kojima (ed.), *Pacific Trade and Development* (reprinted in *Economic Record*, June 1968).

5. See Sperry Lea, 'Free Trade by Sectors', in National Planning Association, *Looking Ahead* (Sep. 1966).

6. F. W. Holmes, 'Australia and New Zealand in the World Economy', *Economic Record* (Mar. 1967).

7. Two conferences were held, one by the Japan Economic Research Center, Tokyo, in January 1968 and one by the East–West Center, Honolulu, in January 1969. A third conference was held in Australia, and a related conference was held in Chile during 1970.

8. Assurance against the reimposition of duties in a free-trade area would induce enterprises to expand trade and investment abroad. The code of good conduct would reduce uncertainty in international trade and be a partial substitute for the formation of a free-trade area. See Balassa, *Trade Liberalization among Industrial Countries*, pp. 160–1.

9. N. P. G. Elkan suggests an interesting scheme for promoting horizontal trade in his article, 'How to Beat Backwash: The Case for Customs-Drawback Unions', *Economic Journal* (Mar. 1965). His plan may be applicable to trade between small economies like Australia and New Zealand, but would be too cumbersome to work in wider markets. It seems to me that horizontal trade would be fostered most efficiently through the expansion of joint ventures and other private investment activities.

10. The Aid Committee could be set up first because of the urgency of increasing aid and trade with developing countries.

11. Maxwell Stamp Associates, op. cit. A counterpart study in America was presented by Franck and Weisband (eds), *A Free Trade Association*.

12. Canadian-American Committee, *A Canada–U.S. Free Trade Arrangement, Survey of Possible Characteristics* (Oct. 1963); *A Possible Plan for Canada–U.S. Free Trade Area, A Staff Report* (Feb. 1965); and *A New Trade Strategy for Canada and the United States* (May 1966).

13. Maxwell Stamp Associates, op. cit., p. 42.

14. This comprises $225 million from the United States market and $43 million from the Canadian market.

15. Maxwell Stamp Associates, op. cit., p. 44.

16. 'If NAFTA actually came into existence Japan would almost certainly be anxious to join it, for she could not contemplate being isolated from a bloc which included the U.S.A. She might find it difficult to meet fully the conditions of participation if NAFTA were to be established in (say) the next five years, but with a steady transformation of agriculture and the modification of traditional social attitudes, the barriers to free trade in agricultural products and to industrial investment by foreigners are likely to crumble.' G. C. Allen, *Japan's Place in Trade Strategy: Larger Role in Pacific Region* (Atlantic Trade Study, London, 1968), pp. 60–1.

17. Maxwell Stamp Associates, op. cit., p. 38.

18. Ibid., p. 78.

19. Lea, loc cit., pp. 40–2.

20. Johnson, in Kojima (ed.), *Pacific Trade and Development*, p. 250.

21. I. A. McDougall, 'Prospects of the Economic Integration of Japan, Australia and New Zealand', in Kojima (ed.), *Pacific Trade and Development*, p. 115.

22. Peter D. Drysdale, 'Japan, Australia, New Zealand: The Prospect for Western Pacific Economic Integration', in Kojima (ed.), *Pacific Trade and Development II*; I. A. McDougall, 'JANFTA and Asian Developing Countries: Sectoral Analysis', ibid.; L. V. Castle, 'Alternative Policies in Trade Cooperation of the Advanced Pacific Countries in the Next Five Years', ibid.

Index

advance cut v. tariff quota preference schemes, 114–17

agreed specialisation: model of, 58–68; in practice, 68–70

agricultural development in Asian developing countries, 129–37

agricultural products, Asian, transfer of markets to, 97–104

agricultural raw materials, 81

agriculture, 10, 12, 24, 44, 94, 171

aid: directly productive, 126–9; fertiliser, scheme for, 129–33

aid-cum-trade preferences: PAFTA and, 137–41; scheme for, 117–20

Asia and 'extended Pacific trade', 74–5

Asian agricultural products, transfer of markets to, 97–104

Asian developing countries, and PAFTA, 121–41; agricultural development, 129–37; aid-cum-trade preferences, 137–41; directly productive aid, 126–9; North–South problem, new stage in, 121–6

Asian developing countries, trade with, 78–80, 81, 167–71

Asian Development Bank, 137, 163

Australia: export–import ratio, 25–8; free trade with New Zealand, 73, 167, 174; global tariff reductions, effect of, 97; gross national product, 174; horizontal-type trade, 88; intensity of trade with, 19, 24, 25–8; intra-areal trade, 75–80, 82–9; and NAFTA, 173–5; and Pacific Currency Area, 146–64; and Pacific economic integration, 51, 71 et seq.; and Pacific Free Trade Area, 49, 71 et seq.; population and income level, 72; and reserve pooling, 150–2; tariff elimination, effects of, 90–95; tariff reduction, effect of, 36; trade

with Asian developing countries, 80, 98–9; vertical-type trade, 82

Austria, quota restrictions, 46

balance of payments, 159–62; iter-areal adjustment, 156–8

Benelux, quota restrictions, 46

bilateral trade, pattern of, 24–8

Brussels Tariff Nomenclature, 44, 46

Canada: Automotive Agreement with United States, 167; exporti–mport ratio, 25–8; global tariff reductions, effect of, 97; horizontal-type trade, 82–3, 86–8; intensity of trade with, 19, 24, 25–8; intra-areal trade, 75–80, 82–9; non-tariff restrictions, 46; and NAFTA, 48–9, 172–3; and Pacific Currency Area, 146–64; and Pacific economic integration, 51, 71 et seq.; population and income level, 72; and reserve pooling, 150–2; tariff elimination, effects of, 90–95; tariff reduction, effect of, 36; trade with developing countries, 98–9; voluntary export quota, 46

capital-intensive goods, 81

cash-crop plantations, programme for, 133–7

Central American Common Market, 68

chemicals, 11, 13, 14, 29–32, 35, 36, 48, 49, 83, 88, 92, 93, 94, 98

China: Communist, 50; mainland, 98, 171

coal, 45

commodity groups, 81–8

cotton, 10, 133, 135–7

Council for Mutual Economic Assistance, 69

customs union theory, 54–8, 148

Denmark, 46

191